To Hope and Back

To Hope and Back

The Journey of the *St. Louis*

KATHY KACER

Second Story Press

Library and Archives Canada Cataloguing in Publication

Kacer, Kathy, 1954-

To hope and back : the journey of the St. Louis / by Kathy Kacer.

(The Holocaust remembrance series for young readers.)

ISBN 978-1-897187-96-8

1. Jewish refugees—Germany—Juvenile literature. 2. Jews—Germany—History—1933-1945—Juvenile literature. 3. St. Louis (Ship)—Juvenile literature. 4. Jewish children in the Holocaust—Juvenile literature. I. Title. II. Series: Holocaust remembrance series for young readers

D804.34.K33 2011   j940.53'18   C2011-904488-9

Edited by Sheba Meland
Cover and text design by Melissa Kaita
Printed and bound in Canada

The views or opinons expressed in this book and the context in which the images are used, do not necessarily reflect the views or policy of, nor imply approval or endorsement by, the United States Holocaust Memorial Museum.

Second Story Press gratefully acknowledges the support of the Ontario Arts Council and the Canada Council for the Arts for our publishing program. We acknowledge the financial support of the Government of Canada through the Canada Book Fund.

ONTARIO ARTS COUNCIL
CONSEIL DES ARTS DE L'ONTARIO

Canada Council   Conseil des Arts
for the Arts   du Canada

MIX
Paper from
responsible sources
FSC   FSC® C004071
www.fsc.org

Published by
SECOND STORY PRESS
20 Maud Street, Suite 401
Toronto, Ontario, Canada
M5V 2M5
www.secondstorypress.ca

"The world seemed to be divided into two parts – those places where the Jews could not live and those where they could not enter."
—Chaim Weizmann[*]

To Lisa Avedon and Sol Messinger
With deep gratitude

Foreword

BY THE SPRING of 1939, Germany had become a very dangerous place for Jews. Adolf Hitler had been the Chancellor since 1933, and his Nuremberg laws had been passed two years after he came to power. This list of anti-Semitic rules was the official policy of Hitler's Nazi party, and outlined the terrible conditions under which Jews were allowed to live. It restricted the basic human and legal rights of all German Jews, and even took away their citizenship.

Dachau, the first concentration camp, had been open since March 1933. The camp was originally designed to imprison Jews as well as German political prisoners – those who were opposed to Hitler's policies. Though the horrific death camps were not yet in operation, Dachau would serve as a model for the many Nazi concentration camps that would follow.

On November 9, 1938, Jewish homes in Nazi Germany and

in parts of Austria were looted and ransacked. More than 1,600 synagogues had their windows smashed, and were set afire. Thirty thousand Jewish men were arrested and taken to concentration camps. This event became known as *Kristallnacht* – the night of broken glass.

All throughout Germany, Jewish people feared for their safety from Nazi discrimination, believing that all of these events – the Nuremberg laws, Kristallnacht, the formation of the concentration camps – were only the beginning of a deliberate plan to wipe out Jews in Germany, and possibly all of Europe. Many tried to leave, but found it difficult to do so. Visas were needed if you wanted to enter another country, and many countries at this time were not eager to accept Jews. They feared that if they did, they would be overrun by a flood of Jewish refugees fleeing Europe.

Germany in May, 1939, was a country on the brink of war, with many Jewish families searching frantically for a safe place to live. But where? And how? This is the true account of a ship's journey to find freedom for its passengers in the midst of these desperate times, and the story of Lisa and Sol, two young people who were aboard that ship, the SS *St. Louis*.

Lisa

THIS MUST BE the biggest ship in the world. It looks longer than our block, and higher than ten houses piled on top of each other. Its hull is black, and there are two tall smokestacks painted in red, white, and black stripes. Mutti says it has six decks, but that those are just the ones we can see above the water. Down below the water line are more levels, where the crew will be sleeping, and where our luggage will be stored. "Our cabin is somewhere near the top," Mutti says, pointing way up high, "along with the other first class passengers."

I should be excited. We are about to sail across the ocean. I should feel my heart pounding in my chest at the thought that we will be at sea for two whole weeks on a journey that will take us very far away from here. Waiting on the pier with us are hundreds of other passengers – mostly Jewish people like me and my family. We all carry documents – visas and other papers that will allow us to enter Havana, the capital city of Cuba, where this ship is bound. I heard Mutti and Oma say these documents are more valuable than all of our luggage and money combined.

Soon after we get to the island of Cuba we will be going on to the United States of America. That's our final destination. Mutti says it's a country where people are happy to welcome Jews like us. All this

The *St. Louis* left Germany from this port in Hamburg.

should make me jump for joy. And yes, I am curious about what this new country will be like. Will America have beautiful old buildings, like the ones in Munich where I am from? Will America have parks and schools where children like me can go, even if we are Jewish? And, most important, will America be free of the Nazi soldiers who have been patrolling Germany looking for Jews to threaten and arrest? They are even here at the port in Hamburg. These soldiers are not on the pier to wave us good-bye with banners wishing us a pleasant voyage. They are here to make sure that we are gone for good. *Judenfrei*, that's what Germany wants to be – free of Jews.

I am not sad to leave these soldiers far behind me.

It is leaving home, probably forever, that makes me sad. I'm afraid I will never see our beautiful apartment on *Elisabeth Strasse* again. Two days ago when I looked out the window of our flat on the fourth floor, I realized that this would be the last time I would see the trolley cars rumble up *Tenk Strasse*, with men, women, and children hanging off the step and out the windows. This would be the last time for me to watch the people rushing by on their way to work, and my last chance to look right across the street to where my grandmother, my Oma Ida, has been living in her apartment for as long as I can remember. At least I don't have to say good-bye to my Oma. She is here, dressed in her traveling clothes, coming with us on this voyage.

I am so sad to leave the *Englischen Garten* behind. Paula, our nanny, has taken me to play in this beautiful park close to my home almost every day since I was born. There are two merry-go-rounds in the park; the big one for grown-ups with giant colorful horses, and the littler one, for children like me. I can't imagine that I will never ride that merry-go-round again. That I will never hear the music playing as I go round in circles that make me dizzy, so dizzy that I feel as if I am still spinning long after the ride is over. Saying good-bye to the Englischen Garten was hard for me. But saying good-bye to Paula was even harder.

"You won't forget me," Paula cried as she pulled me close and squeezed me into the warm folds of her body. I knew how dangerous it had become for Christians like Paula to work for Jewish families like

Lisa as a young girl

ours. But Paula never cared about the danger to her or to her family. She has always loved us like we were her own. She has loved *me*.

"Never," I said, muffling my tears against her apron. "Maybe you will visit us in America?"

Paula nodded, but I think that was only to make me feel better. Mutti stood close by, watching me say good-bye to Paula, and not saying a word. But I know how painful it is for Mutti to be leaving Paula behind. Oma used to say Mutti and Paula were almost like sisters. I'm not sure we will see Paula again, and I can feel a lump at the back of my throat.

The gangplank is ready and open. It's time to board the giant ship. "Come, Liselotte," Mutti calls to me. She takes my hand and pulls me toward Shed 76, a building where we show officers the documents that allow us to leave Germany and travel to freedom. Oma Ida is right behind us, with my brother, Phillip. Photographers are snapping pictures of the passengers as we make our way up the broad gangplank. I don't know why. Perhaps the Nazis will celebrate the departure of hundreds of Jews when these pictures appear in the newspapers. All the way up the gangplank Mutti keeps repeating how excited and happy she is to be leaving Germany, but her face tells another story. I see the worry in her eyes, and the disappointment that has taken the sparkle out of her. Yes, she is also scared about this journey, just like me.

The last thing Mutti did before we left our apartment was to snip the yellow Stars of David off each piece of our clothing. "We won't need to wear these anymore," she said as she picked at the black thread that had held the cloth stars in place. It was not so long ago that I had watched her and Oma sew the stars onto our jackets, blouses, and coats. Once we are out of Germany we won't have to be branded as Jews by wearing these stars. We won't have to worry that people on the street will call us names and bully us because of our religion.

There will be four of us in our cabin: me, Mutti, Oma, and my big brother. We always shared a room at home. I love Phillip – he is, after all, my brother – but these days he barely talks to me. He was born with crossed eyes, and I think he is angry because people tease him. With all the growing hatred of Jews, this has been happening a lot. Mutti said we must be strong when we are being chased and

Passengers on board the *St. Louis* look out at the German shore before the ship's departure for Cuba.

called names on the streets. But Phillip has been picked on twice as much – not only because we're Jewish and have to wear the yellow star, but because of his looks, too. I also wonder if the reason Phillip doesn't talk much is because he feels alone. He is the only boy in our family now. I miss my Papa so much it hurts, and I have a feeling that Phillip must miss Papa even more.

The story of my Papa's death is terribly sad, so sad that I get very upset just thinking about it. Papa worked in the family business that my grandfather owned. Mutti always said proudly that Berger und Röckel was the largest greeting card factory in Germany. We heard often at the dinner table that more than nine hundred people worked in the business that was the pride and joy of my family. Papa did a lot of traveling for the company, selling cards and catalogues in other countries in Europe. Because of all the hatred of Jews, he also used these business trips to smuggle our money out of the country, in case we needed to leave.

One of the greeting cards produced by Berger und Röckel

"You never know what might happen here in Germany," he used to say to us. "Hitler and his soldiers are making all kinds of problems for Jews. I'm creating a nest egg for us in Holland, just in case." I didn't even know what a nest egg was until Mutti explained to Phillip and me that it was the kind of savings that you put away for safe keeping until you need it one day in the future. He was so wise, my Papa, thinking ahead like that, even though what he was doing was very dangerous. He whispered to us that it was against the law for Jews to have bank accounts in other countries, but he had to take the risk.

On one of those business trips, the horrible Gestapo – the secret police of the Nazi Party – boarded the train on which Papa was traveling. Any contact with the Gestapo was terribly frightening. Oma told me once they had absolute power of life and death. They searched my father and all the other Jews, and they discovered his bankbooks from Holland, the ones that showed our nest egg. Papa could have been arrested on the spot, but he managed to avoid being taken. Everyone always said that Papa was so charming that he could talk his way out of any situation, and that's what he must have done with the officials. He arrived safely in Holland. But he knew he would never, ever be able to return to us in Germany. He must have missed us so much there in Holland, all alone, believing he might never see us again.

That's when he took his own life. It's as if the Nazis killed him. That's what I think. They made him so sad about what would become of his life that he had no choice but to end it.

SOL

THERE'S A BAND here, playing lively German folk songs. My parents say it's here to send us off on our journey. So we've stopped right in front of the musicians to listen for a minute, even though I am itching to get on the ship.

"Is it time to board yet?" I ask. Papa is holding my hand tightly so that I won't run anywhere. But I am tugging on his arm, trying to get to the gangplank.

"Soon," my Papa replies. "Be still, Salo."

I gaze up, up, and up the full height of the ocean liner, straining to see the top deck, and down the hull, as long as two soccer fields. I know how long a soccer field is, even though I'm not very good at sports. I am small, like my father. My strength is in my brain. That's what my Papa says. He taught me how to read and write in Hebrew even before I had started school.

Sol, as an infant, with his parents

Papa is a tailor. He came to Germany from Poland years ago. The tailor shop where he worked with his brother, Adolf, was below us, in the same building where we lived. I used to spend time there almost every day with my cousin Simi, Uncle Adolf and Aunt Genia's daughter. In one corner of the shop was a platform where people would stand to try on the suits and coats that Papa and Uncle Adolf were making for them. Simi and I would sit on the platform and pick out the "practise" threads that were in the fabric, the ones that held the garment together until the final sewing was complete. That was our job, and I would pretend I was going to be a tailor just like my father. The work was fun – and the other employees would give me and Simi candy when we were done; that was the best part. Those are my good memories of Berlin and home. But we've left all that behind to travel by train here to Hamburg, for a long voyage across the sea.

Sol's father and mother

"Is our cabin way up there?" I point to a deck that is about a hundred feet above where we are, looking up from the pier. I am jumping with excitement, and trying to pull my parents along, but they don't seem to be in any hurry. Papa shakes his head and points to a round porthole just above the water.

"The higher decks are for the rich people. We'll stay on a lower deck with the other third class passengers. We're lucky to get passage at all," he adds, giving my Mutti and me a look full of joy and relief.

And I know he is right.

The first time I remember what it felt like to be Jewish and different was when I was only four years old. Every Saturday morning, on the Sabbath, our day of rest and prayer, Mutti and Papa would take me to the park near the corner of *Legiendamm* and *Leuschnerdamm*, a short stroll from our home in Berlin. I couldn't wait for that walk, mostly because we would meet up with my cousin, Edith, and her parents, Uncle Adolf and Aunt Frieda. Yes, I have two Uncle Adolfs – but they couldn't be more different. Edith's father is very kind and speaks in a quiet voice, while my other Uncle Adolf, the one who works with Papa, is more nervous and strict. Imagine that my two Jewish uncles have the same first name as the man who hates Jews, Adolf Hitler! I guess their parents couldn't look into the future.

Edith is one year older than me, and she's not only my cousin, but also one of my best friends. Our parents would sit on one of the park benches, while Edith and I played, running across the lawns and around the giant oak trees. Edith always wore a big, white bow in her hair that would flop around as we ran from one end of the park to the other. I could pick Edith out in a crowd anywhere, just because of that big, white bow. After playing, we would choose our own bench where we would sit and talk – just the two of us, away from the grown-ups.

Then one day, everything changed. A law was passed and the park benches were painted new colors, yellow for Jews, and green for every-one else.

"We can't sit here anymore, Shloimele," my mother said the next time we met Edith and her family at the park. "We must sit here now." She pointed to one of the freshly painted yellow benches.

Now Edith and I had a choice. We could sit on a yellow bench and be made fun of by the German children for

Sol could always spot his cousin Edith by the big, white bow she wore in her hair.

being Jewish, or we could stand and pretend none of this mattered. I made a different choice. After that, I didn't want to go to the park anymore. Even though I was only four, I understood that this law was aimed at Jews – to separate us from everyone else, to single us out. The law was aimed at *me*.

And that was only the beginning. After that, everything became more dangerous for us. We couldn't shop in this store, or eat in that restaurant, or go the cinema, or even walk alone on the street. That last one wasn't exactly a law. But if you walked alone, there was a good chance you would be attacked by gangs eager to beat up Jews, for no reason except our religion. The police did nothing about it. They stood by and watched: seeing people hit us and tear our clothes was entertaining for them. I couldn't even play in the courtyard of our apartment building, because Mutti was afraid that the German children might punch me. That happened once, and after that, the courtyard was off limits for me. I watched Mutti become more and more nervous. I had never seen her like this before.

But who could blame her? After Papa was arrested, I was all she had.

It happened on October 28, 1938. We were all sleeping when there was a loud knock at the door. You know when there is a pounding like that in the middle of the night it must be trouble. No one comes in the middle of the night with good news. I crept out of my bed to watch from behind a door in the living room, and saw two Gestapo police enter the apartment. They ordered Papa to dress quickly.

"Where are you taking him?" Mutti cried out. She had gotten out of bed so quickly that she didn't even have time to brush her long, dark hair into place. Wisps flew in all directions.

"Shut up! It's none of your business!" one of the officers barked. By now I was crying. I ran to stand next to my mother and then I began screaming for the men not to take my father away.

"If you don't shut that kid up, I'm going to kill him," the other officer said.

He said it as calmly as that, as if the possibility of killing someone, even a boy like me, was an everyday event. That was when Mutti leaned down and placed her hand over my mouth. She held it there, muffling my screams, while the Gestapo men led Papa from our house.

The next morning Mutti and I went to the police station. There were dozens, maybe hundreds of women and children crowding together, all trying to get information about their men, who had also been taken in the middle of the night. No one wanted to ask too many questions, because the police might single them out and take them too. So we all waited and listened for any news. Mutti's face still showed the shock from the night before. My mother is usually so calm and dignified. But on this morning her face was pasty white, and her hands shook as she held mine.

Finally, an announcement was made. "All Jewish men of Polish citizenship have been shipped back to Poland." That was all the information we got, and there was nothing we could do about it except to return to our apartment, alone, just Mutti and me.

It took several weeks before we got a letter from Papa in Poland. During that time, Mutti was terribly nervous. I could barely look at her face. The fear was everywhere – in her eyes, her mouth, which became tight and set, and her shoulders, which hunched up around her ears. And I became scared along with her. She tried to tell me that Papa would be fine, that *we* would be fine, but it was hard to believe her. Hitler had ordered all of the Polish Jews out of Germany. I was pretty sure that soon, he would want to get rid of all of the German Jews as well. And that would mean us.

When Papa's first letter finally came, he explained that after arriving in Poland, he had gone to the city of Cracow and had begun to work there as a tailor. "I will try to send money to the two of you so that you can manage while I'm gone. Be strong, the letter said. "I am doing everything I can to get papers so that we can get to safety – together."

We have three suitcases that we are taking with us out of Germany – hardly anything compared to the many steamer trunks, crates, and piles of luggage that sit on the pier like little buildings lined up in a row. Those must be the belongings that the rich passengers are taking with them. The truth is, we have very little left. While my Papa was away from us in Poland, Mutti had to sell off our possessions for next to nothing. Some of the money went to buy us food. But she told me that she was putting some aside to pay for a way out of the country.

In October, my Uncle Adolf, Aunt Genia, and cousin Simi left for the United States of America. They were so lucky to get papers to go there. Mutti and I went to the train station with them to say good-bye. Mutti was crying, and she told them it was partly because she was so sad to see them go, and partly because she longed for us all to be traveling with them. I could see Simi's face, a face I saw nearly every day, in the window of the train as it pulled away. I was trying to be very brave and not cry. The last thing I remember was her hand waving to me.

By December, Edith and her parents had also left Germany. They, too, were lucky and managed to get visas for the island of Cuba.

"You'll come soon," Edith had said, the night she and her parents came to say good-bye to us. "It's just taking a little longer for your papers." Edith is always so kind, just like her father. I knew she was trying to make me feel better, and I hoped she was right. "It's so much harder to organize things because your father isn't here," she added. "But you'll come too, and in the meantime, I'll find a park in Cuba for us – we'll play!"

Aunt Rose, my father's sister, was living with us. I shared the living room of our tiny apartment with her; she slept on the couch and me on a small cot that we rolled out every night. Even Aunt Rose managed to get her papers for Cuba before we did. She showed me her passport when she was packing her suitcase for the train that would take her to Hamburg where she would board a ship. All I remember is the red letter "J" stamped next to her name – the bright color nearly jumping off the page. There was no mistaking that she was a Jewish traveler. When Aunt Rose left, Mutti looked like she felt more alone that ever, even though I hugged her and told her she still had me.

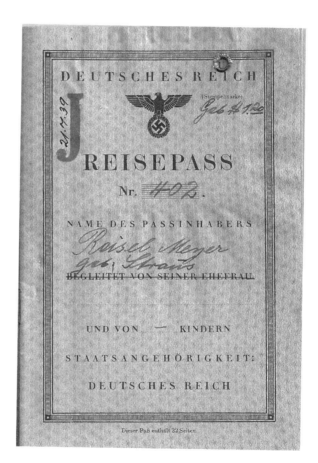

Aunt Rose's passport was stamped with the letter, "J," marking her as a Jew. Her full name was Reisel Meyer.

Edith was right about the papers. It took longer for Papa to help arrange things from Cracow, but he did it! Finally, a letter arrived, saying that our landing permits to Cuba were waiting for us at the German emigration office in Berlin. I went there with Mutti, lining up with other scared-looking Jewish families. The German official behind the desk was not friendly. He barely looked at Mutti and

me. In fact, when he finally raised his eyes to glance at us, his mouth twisted in disgust, as if he couldn't stand being this close to us. He shoved the papers at Mutti, she grabbed them, and we fled from that office, relieved when we were finally back in our flat, papers in hand. Mutti, Papa, and I could now sail to Cuba.

But the day before we were due to leave for the port in Hamburg, there was still no sign of my father.

"What will we do if he doesn't come back in time, Mutti?" I asked.

She shook her head. "He wrote me that if he isn't here, we must leave without him."

At this, she turned her face away. I stood there not saying a word, but inside, my stomach was turning in sick circles. I could not imagine leaving without my Papa. I went to the living room and slumped on my cot, shaking even though it was not cold. Our three cases stood packed at the front door, ready to leave with us at the crack of dawn. Mutti had said over and over that we were going to a place where we would be safe and free. There would be no gangs waiting to beat up Jewish kids. There would be no park benches where I was forbidden to sit. But all I could think about was that I didn't want to leave without my Papa. How could this freedom be worth it, if we were not going to be together?

You won't believe this, but late that night came another sudden knock at the door. I could hear my Mutti shrieking. I ran to join her. Was it the Gestapo again? But Mutti's face was lit up as if she knew

An eager Sol walked up the gangway to
the *St. Louis* with his mother behind him.

that knock and knew who was waiting behind the door. She opened it…and there was Papa! We had not seen him in seven months. He was thinner than I remembered, and his face was pale. My Papa has a scar across one eye from an accident he had years ago. The mark stood out even more on his sickly, thin face. He almost looked like a stranger. But when he smiled and gathered me into his arms I knew for sure that it was Papa. He had come back to us. I tried to ask him about Poland; what had it been like there? That night he wouldn't answer me, and I have never asked him since.

So here we are today, about to board this ocean liner for our voyage to a new life. Someone has just taken a picture of us as we walk up the long gangplank. We are passing under the giant Nazi flag flapping in the breeze, I hope it's the last time that I have to look at that ugly thing with its blood-red background and the swastika, that thick, black cross with the bent arms. I am so excited to be going on this journey across the ocean. We will meet Edith and her parents in Cuba, and then we will all go to the United States. But what makes me want to shout with joy is that we are together, me, Papa, and Mutti. No one has been left behind.

Lisa

TODAY AS we walked up the gangplank, I realized it was Saturday. I remembered how much I loved going with my family to the *Hauptsynagoge*, the main synagogue in Munich, every Saturday morning. I would sit with Mutti and my grandmother in the women's section, while Phillip and Papa sat below us with the other men. As soon as we sat down, Oma would open her prayer book and begin to read, following along with Rabbi Baerwald who was leading the service. Oma swayed slightly, side to side, reciting the blessings that were important to her while I watched, wondering if one of the prayers was for me.

Her prayers would last only for a couple of minutes. After that, she would shut the prayer book and sit back. That was the cue I was waiting for, and I would lean in close to her and to Mutti. And then, until the service was over, she and Mutti would whisper together about

Lisa's grandmother,
Oma Ida

the other people in the synagogue.

"You see poor Mrs. Abelsdorff over there? Her daughter – who knows if she'll ever marry. Twenty-one years old and still not a bride."

"And what about Mrs. Kaufmann? I hear her son was going to be a rabbi, but now he's not so sure. It's breaking her heart."

Back and forth the comments flew while I listened, stretching my neck to see who they were pointing to. They never said anything hurtful about anyone. This was just their time to catch up on local gossip – the news of the week. And for me, their chitchat was much more interesting than the slow prayers going on below. The only time Oma would stop talking and listen was when the cantor sang some of the most beautiful prayers near the end of the service. My grandmother loves the music of the operas. I was practically raised on the sound of that music played on the big phonograph in her sitting room. And while her opera records were spinning around on the phonograph, no one was allowed to speak or even move. She wanted us to listen carefully to the "heavenly music," as she called it. I think that some of the beautiful Hebrew prayers remind my grandmother of her beloved operas.

We have the phonograph with us on the ship. It is somewhere deep down in the hold, along with all the other belongings that we have brought from our home. There are huge crates filled with the furniture from our flat, paintings, crystal wine decanters, and even Mutti's fancy, hand-painted bone china dinner set that serves twelve people. Our belongings will come with us, first to Cuba and then to America, where they will fill the rooms of a new home.

"It is as if we are bringing a little bit of Germany with us," Mutti says. "It will remind us of the life we once had."

Our cabin is small compared to our flat in Munich, but as nice as Mutti said it would be. The carpeting on the floor is thick and velvety. The lights in the sitting room glow softly. Oma says the stewards will come each night and turn down the beds with their rich, embroidered bedspreads and silky, pale sheets. There is a large bed on one side of the room for Mutti and Oma and a bunk bed on the other side. Right away my brother climbs into the top bunk. We didn't discuss which bed would be his and which would be mine, but that's fine. I like my bottom bunk. It's a dark, quiet cocoon, my private space. It is a perfect place for my dolls. I've brought two with me on this voyage. Both of them have porcelain faces, and wear fancy silk dresses that I dressed them in for the trip. One of my dolls has long, brown braids. My hair is short. But one day I will grow it long and braid it just like my doll's.

I've also brought books – some of my favorites, including *Madeline* by Ludwig Bemelmans. I've read it dozens of times, but

Paintings, furniture, and crystal were just some of the items Lisa's family brought with them on the *St. Louis*.

that doesn't matter. By the time this voyage is over, I will have read it dozens more! My books and my dolls will keep me company for the next two weeks. Mutti says there will be other children on board, but I'm not so interested in that. Sometimes I am shy with new children. I will read, dress my dolls, and dream about what our lives will be like in Cuba and then this big country called the United States of America. Besides, Mutti is here to keep me company and so is Oma, and maybe Phillip too, if he comes out of his shell. They will be my friends on the journey across the ocean.

Once we have unpacked, Mutti says we must go up on deck so we can watch as the ship leaves the pier. I don't want to leave our cabin just yet. I need to settle my dolls into the bunk just right – so that they will be comfortable for the long trip. But Mutti is calling me.

"Come, Liselotte. It will be your last time to look at the shores of Germany," she says.

So I put my dolls and books aside and join her and my grandmother and Phillip. We hurry along with the hundreds of other passengers. Some, like us, are dressed in their best travel clothes. Others look as if their jackets and pants are very old, and their shoes are shabby. There are religious families – the men with long beards, women with their hair covered by scarves, and little boys running with their long earlocks of curled hair flying. And there are families with children who look just like me. Oma says to Mutti, "Can you believe that almost every single passenger on this ship is Jewish? We have never been in such a huge crowd of Jewish families, not even on the High Holy days at our synagogue."

Mostly, everyone looks happy. I guess all of these Jewish families are relieved to be leaving Germany. But I can see several women who are crying. And the children who are standing next to them look

Many postcards like this one were produced of the *St. Louis.*

frightened, as if they have lost their parents, even though they are right there.

"Hello, young *Fräulein*. Is there anything that I can get for you?" A man is speaking, and at first I don't realize that he is talking to me, and calling me "young miss." My mother prods me gently. "No thank you, *mein Herr*," I reply with equal politeness. "I am fine, sir."

The man smiles and winks before he turns and moves on to the next passenger. He is one of the stewards. I can see other sailors and crewmembers carrying suitcases for passengers, helping some of the elderly, and bringing around big silver trays of drinks, which they offer to everyone on deck. Each of these crewmembers is polite and friendly. They bow and speak very formally to the passengers, calling them "mister" and "miss." I hear a lady next to me say that she has not had such kind treatment in months. Jews have been singled out, made fun of, and even jailed, just because of their religion – *my* religion. But not any more.

"We are finally going to be treated like real people," my grandmother says. She smiles and proudly lifts her head. She is so beautiful, my Oma – so dignified – everyone says so. And she never looks as sad as Mutti does, even though my Opa, her husband, died many years ago. I guess she's had more time to get used to being without him. After so many years alone, sadness gets softer, she told me once.

Suddenly, I see an important-looking man walking toward us on the deck. He is wearing a fine black uniform, with gold braid on the

F

I. Klasse

Falkenstein	Max ū/3
	Hilda 3
	Werner xxv7/12
Feig	Eva Sara xx7//1
Finkelstein	
Fischer	Johanna xxv7/k1
	Hans-Hermann 22
"	Ruth 138
Fraenkel	Hans xiv7/99
Frank	Manfred IX7/84
Freiberg	Reula Regina 7X/34
	Herta 35
	Gisela 36
Freund	Terese xv7/9
	Philipp 20
	Lieselotte 21
Fried	Engelbert iii7/78
Friedheim	Alfred xiv7/i
	Hertha 12
Friedmann	Amalie
"	Bruno
"	Georg
"	Lillian
Fuchs-Marx	Walther xiv7/3i
	Anna 32
Fuld	Julie xiv7/52
"	Ludwig 5
"	Hans 59
Fried	Engelbert xxviii7/

Tour. Klasse

Falk	Eugen n7/4c
Fanto	Julius vii7/20 L
Feilchenfeld	Alice xiii7/14
"	Kind 2/4ec 18
"	Wolf 15
"	Berta 16
"	Heinz 17
Fink	Manfred n7/10a
"	Herta 6
"	Michael c
Fischbach	Jonas n7/68
"	Amalia 67
"	Moritz 66
"	Amalia 69
Flamberg	Braudla n7/29a
	Fella 6
Fränkel	Leon vii7/9a
	Alice 6
Frank	Max xi7/i
"	Moritz v7/8a
"	Clara 6
"	Ursula c
"	Siegfried xiv7/3
Frankfurter	Lilly xxii7/8
Friedemann	Walter iii7/104
Friedheim	Edith x7/21
Friedmann	Rosi xiii7/2
"	Eva-Ruth 6
"	Willy v7/
Fröhlich	Max x7/24
	30

I. Klasse

Gabel	Heinrich xvii7/14
	Beate 95
	Gerhard 96
Gabitz	Max xii7/9
"	Martha 10
"	Heinz 11
Glade	Bruno xxviii7/ii
Glass	Herbert 18/ii
Glücksmann	Hans xxviii7/22
"	Margarete 28
Goldbaum	Anna iv7/86
Goldberg	Wilhelm xxvi7/76
Goldschmidt	Adolf xxiv7/89
"	Gerda 50
"	Inge 57
"	Lore 52
Gottschalk	Jacob xii7/3
"	Regina 4
"	Erika 5
"	Charlotte 6
Grünstein	Heinz iii7/43
"	Gerd 44
Grünthal	Else xiii7/42
"	Walter xi7/7
"	Margarete 8
"	Ruthild 9
"	Sibyll 10
"	Wolf Adolf 11
"	Bertha 12
"	Lutz 13
"	Horst 14
Gutmann	Martha xvii7/6i
Guttmann	Sally 18/45
Guttmann	Ruth 46
	Jr

Tour. Klasse

Gelband	Benjamin xvi7/ii5
	Chana 116
Gerber	Rosa xiv7/90
"	Ruth 91
Gimenez Espinosa	José
Glaser	Arthur I7/10
Glaserfeld	Max v7/10a
Glücksmann	Heinrich iii7/189
Goldreich	Rudolf iv7/ii
	Therese 120
Goldschmidt	Alex v7/5c
"	Helmut c
"	Else xi7/1
"	Fritz 2
Goldstein	Hermann xvii7/9i
"	Recha Rita 92
"	Heinz 13
Gottfeld	Julius I7/38
	Rosa I7/39
Gotthelf	Fritz xvii7/5
	Käte 6
Gottlieb	Sally I7/2
Greilsamer	Erich xv7/6
Greve	Walter iii7/1
"	Johanna 2
"	Heinz 3
"	Eveline 4

shoulders of his high-buttoned jacket. He has a black naval cap on his head. The shocking thing is that with his small, dark moustache he looks a little bit like Adolf Hitler, at least from the pictures that I have seen of him. But I know the man in front of me is not Hitler. This man has a kind face. He walks confidently and quickly, with his hands clasped behind his back, and nods ever so slightly to the passengers.

"The captain, Liselotte!" my mother whispers. But she doesn't need to tell me this. He is not very tall, but he looks as if he is the most important person on the ship. The stewards and other crewmen salute him as he passes, and the crowd of passengers moves aside to let him go by. I watch as he climbs the stairs. Philip explains to us that the captain is going to the bridge, the upper deck where he will take the helm. It seems Phillip has been studying up on all these sailing terms. He says the captain is ready to take command of the ship, and sail her with the help of his crew. Our lives are in his hands now.

I feel some slight motion beneath me. We're leaving! I press up against the railing to watch the SS *St. Louis* glide away from the pier and begin to sail out to sea. A loud horn blasts, and the people on deck start to cheer. "We're moving, Mutti!" I scream. It is 8:00 p.m., the end of the Sabbath on Saturday, May 13, 1939.

LEFT: The names of the Freund family – Lisa, Phillip, and their mother – are seen on this part of the ship's passenger list.

SOL

I CAN SEE the lights of Hamburg growing dimmer and fainter as the *St. Louis* slowly moves out of the harbor. For an ocean liner so big, I am surprised at how smoothly we are leaving the port. The ship moves as if it is sliding on ice. It reminds me of the time we went on vacation to the North Sea. So many of my relatives were there; my aunts, my two Uncle Adolfs, my cousin Simi, my Aunt Rose, and others. Edith and I paddled in a small rowboat that cut through the waves of the sea with barely a roll, just like the *St. Louis* as it sails out of the harbor. That was in happier times, when we never dreamed we would be running away from Germany in this giant ship. I wonder if the sailing will be as smooth once we are out in the open sea.

Truthfully, I don't really care if the trip gets bumpy, or if we sail into a storm, I am just happy to be getting away. I think I have lived in Germany for too long already. I have seen enough of the troubles here. My mind flashes back once more to the awful weeks and months before today. On November 9, one week after Papa was taken away, I woke up to discover from Mutti that I would not be going to school that day...

"Terrible things happened last night while you were sleeping, Shloimele. You're staying home with me today," she said as I walked into the kitchen. Mutti was sitting at the table, still in her nightclothes. "I don't know how you slept through it. But I'm glad you did," she added quickly, looking up with worried eyes.

"What happened? Why is there no school today?" I ran to the window to look out at the street. It looked as if an earthquake had hit Berlin. Of course I have never actually seen an earthquake, except in magazine pictures, or in newsreels that play at the cinema. But that's what this looked like. Broken bottles, rocks, and other garbage lay across the streets and sidewalks outside my apartment. Dozens of windows on the buildings across the street were broken into pieces. And dark clouds of smoke hung across the city, where fires were still blazing.

"They are saying it was a raid targeted at Jews across Germany," Mutti said as she came to stand next to me. "They are calling it 'the night of broken glass,' because so many buildings had their windows shattered in the night. We are lucky that we are safe. I've heard that thousands of Jewish men were arrested. No one knows where they've been taken." Even though Mutti sounded calm as she spoke, I could tell she was anything but. I knew Mutti was very scared. My mind jumped immediately to Papa. We still had not heard from him. We had no idea where he had been taken, or even whether he was still alive.

A few days later, Mutti received word that my school had re-opened, and I could now go back to class. We walked there together that morning, saying nothing. Mutti clutched my hand tightly in hers, and pulled me along nervously. In the days since the attack, the city had cleaned up the broken glass and garbage that had littered the streets. Kids were playing tag and laughing on the way to school, and the traffic roared along as usual. On the surface, things once again seemed as if they had returned to normal. But to me, "normal" was already beginning to feel like a strange word. Normal these days meant being without Papa. It meant that Jews could be bullied and arrested for no reason. For some, Berlin might have returned to normal, but everything felt completely *abnormal* to me.

And then we reached my school. My school stands next to the synagogue where I used to go every Saturday morning with my Papa – until he was taken away. I had such happy memories of walking to the synagogue with my father. He would ask me questions about what I was learning in school, and then we would talk about our vacation in the North Sea and when we might return there with the whole family. On this morning as Mutti and I approached the school, I could smell the wreckage even before we turned the corner and saw the destruction. The synagogue had been burned right to the ground.

All that remained was smoking rubble, and a horrible smell of burnt wood and cloth that filled the air and scorched my throat and my nostrils. Mutti and I coughed and coughed, standing there in shock.

"Perhaps it's a good thing that your papa is not here to see what's become of our beautiful place of worship." Mutti's voice was quiet and bitter sounding.

And once more, I could see how much the Jews of my city were hated; *I* was hated.

That's why I'm so relieved that we're all here on the deck of the *St. Louis,* watching the Hamburg pier grow smaller in the distance. I almost want to whoop with joy and shake my fist at the shore. But something stops me. Papa is crying next to me.

"All of our relatives," Papa says as tears stream down his cheeks. "There are still so many left behind. God only know when – or if – we will ever see them again."

Mutti is crying too, but I think she is as thankful as I am, and her tears are those of relief. That's what I can feel as I watch the last lights of Germany flicker in the distance and then disappear. Now there is just the darkness of the sea. This soft blackness feels so much safer than the lights we've left behind. The ship is picking up speed, and a cool breeze is beginning to blow across my face. The sky is so clear that it looks as if there are millions of stars above me. I can smell salt in the sea air, mixed in with something good that is being prepared in the dining rooms below. I take a deep breath, and let it out slowly.

WHAT THE CAPTAIN KNEW

ANTI-SEMITISM – the senseless hatred of and discrimination against innocent Jews – had been present in Europe and in other parts of the world for many years. But in the 1930s, under Adolf Hitler and his Nazi Party, anti-Semitism was on a steep rise in Germany. It was against this backdrop of naked hostility against Jews that Captain Gustav Schroeder climbed to the bridge of a German ship in Hamburg called the SS *St. Louis* and readied it to set sail. The ship, part of the Hamburg-American Line (Hapag), was a grand, luxurious ocean liner, six stories high. The 937 passengers on board were mostly Jewish and the captain's orders were to sail the ship to Havana, Cuba, where these passengers would disembark. Captain Schroeder was told to expect 899 Jews, fleeing from Nazi-controlled Germany, to board in Hamburg. He was then to proceed to Cherbourg, France to pick up 38 more Jews. Six of the passengers – a couple from Cuba and four

Captain Gustav Schroeder
was determined to provide
a safe and pleasant passage
for his Jewish passengers.

people from Spain – were not Jewish. They had simply bought passage on the ship and would travel along with everyone else.

All of the Jewish passengers were carrying permits allowing them to enter Cuba. Most of the passengers had bought these permits at a very high fee, from the Director of Immigration for Cuba, a man named Manuel Benitez. It was said that much of the money for the landing permits made its way into Benitez's own pockets. For everyone on board, however, it was worth the price. These precious documents would allow them to enter Cuba, though most hoped that they would eventually make their way to the United States. In fact, 734 of the passengers on board also had visas to the United States. But since there was a limit, called a quota, on the number of Jews or other immigrants allowed into the U.S., each visa had a quota number on it. Visa holders had to wait for their numbers to come up before they would be allowed to enter the country – and that could take anywhere from three months to three years. That's why the Cuban documents were essential. Visa holders would wait in Cuba until their numbers came up.

Many of the travelers on board were wealthy, though a greater number had barely managed to scrape together the money necessary to leave the country. Some had even been released or had escaped from Dachau concentration camp, and were fleeing captivity. The price for a ticket on the *St. Louis* was high. The 400 first class passengers on board had paid 800 Reichsmarks per person, or about $250, the equivalent of $4,000 today. The 500 tourist class passengers had paid 600

Reichsmarks each. Each passenger had to pay an additional 230 Reichsmarks for the return voyage. Of course, none of them intended to ever return to Germany, but this money had to be paid in advance. It would be held in a German bank account, and in truth, the passengers would never see that money again. But that didn't matter to any of them. What mattered was that they were leaving the terrors of Nazi Germany far behind.

Captain Schroeder was a strong and energetic officer. He hated the Nazis, and disapproved of what Hitler was trying to do to innocent Jews. The lives of all passengers on board were always in the hands of a ship's captain. But Captain Schroeder took the responsibility of providing safe passage for his Jewish passengers out of Germany very seriously. He called together all 231 of the SS *St. Louis* crew and instructed them to treat these passengers with the same kind of respect that they would show to the German high society. He knew that

Passengers traveling in third class, like Sol and his parents, had to show this kind of boarding pass.

HAMBURG-AMERIKA LINIE

(Compañía Hamburguesa Americana)

No. 2033

Touristenklasse
Clase Turista
Tourist Class

Motorschiff
motonave
motor vessel } St. Louis

am
d salir
sailing } 13. Mai 1939

von
de
from } Hamburg

nach
á
to } Havana

Name des Reisenden:
nombre del pasajero:
passenger's name:

Herr Dr. Walter Weissler

Bezahlter Fahrpreis
Pasaje pagado — Fare paid

most of the Jewish passengers probably had not been treated well in a very long time. After navigating out of the harbor of Hamburg, the captain recorded the following entry in his diary:

> *There is a somewhat nervous disposition among the passengers. Despite this, everyone seems convinced they will never see Germany again. Touching departure scenes have taken place. Many seem light of heart, having left their homes. Others take it heavily. But beautiful weather, pure sea air, good food, and attentive service will soon provide the usual worry-free atmosphere of long sea voyages. Painful impressions on land disappear quickly at sea and soon seem merely like dreams.*[1]

Like Captain Schroeder, who was happy to sail his passengers away, Nazi Germany was also pleased to see these hundreds of Jews leave its borders. Unlike the captain, Nazi Germany was not interested in the safety of these Jewish passengers. Germany was intent on becoming Judenfrei – free of Jews. But Germany did not want the world to know what fate awaited the Jews who remained in the country. Plans were already in the works for the Nazis' Final Solution – the mass killing of European Jews. Until this plan could be put into place, Germany was willing to let some Jews go. A number of countries were already questioning the treatment of Jews within German borders, so the Nazi government flooded the newsreels and newspapers with reports that it was being good to Jewish families by allowing them to leave on the *St. Louis*.

At the same time, Germany wanted to spread anti-Semitism so it didn't want any other country to welcome these Jewish refugees. Unbeknownst to Captain Schroeder or anyone else on board, the German government was using propaganda, or misleading information, to make sure that the Cuban government and its citizens would never allow the passengers of the *St. Louis* to enter the country.

The photographers who were at the port in Hamburg, snapping pictures of Jewish men, women, and children as they boarded the ship, were told to take pictures of only the most ragged looking and poorest Jews who were boarding. They hoped to show that those who were leaving were "undesirable, criminal elements." Shortly after the *St. Louis*'s departure, Germany released a series of radio and newspaper articles and cinema newsreels stating that the departing Jewish passengers were fleeing from Germany with stolen goods and money. While Captain Schroeder piloted his ship through Hamburg harbor, public demonstrations were already taking place in Havana, aimed at preventing any Jews from landing.

The Jewish passengers on board the ship didn't know anything about the Nazi plans. They were all hoping to leave their troubles behind them in Germany and to enjoy the warmth and hospitality that Captain Schroeder was offering them on board the *St. Louis* as they sailed to the freedom that awaited them across the ocean.

Lisa

I'M STARTING to feel sick! Last night I went to bed still excited. The soft pitch and roll of the ship lulled me into a deep sleep. I even dreamed of the hotel in Hamburg where we stayed for one night before boarding the *St. Louis*. The hotel had an elevator operated by a man in a red uniform. "Stand back, *meine Damen und Herren*, ladies and gentlemen," he ordered as we stepped inside. Once we had moved to the back of the elevator, he unfolded the metal grate of the door, and pulled the lever to lock it, and then he cranked the wheel for the fifth floor where we were staying. I had never been in an elevator, and I wondered at the shiny brass fittings and soft light from the little chandelier above my head. Riding up was like being on the merry-go-round in the Englischen Garten, and I squealed at the moment of weightlessness as the elevator reached our floor and gently rocked into place.

But when I awoke this morning, after dreaming of the elevator, I realized that I still was going up and down! The ship, which began its voyage so smoothly and steadily, has now begun to sway and heave. And my stomach is doing the same. I cannot face breakfast, but after getting dressed, I try to walk on the deck next to Oma, who is holding my hand.

"Stare at the horizon," she says matter-of-factly. "That will help make you feel better."

It is a crystal clear morning. The sun shimmers and sparkles off the ocean. The horizon is a straight line in the far distance where the green sea meets the perfect blue sky. I try to avoid looking at the waves pounding up against the hull of the ship. Instead, I stare and stare at that distant solid line, just as Oma told me to. Sometimes my grandmother is so strict, like when she used to cook for us, and nothing was allowed to remain on our plates. She's never been one to kiss and hug me, but I can tell that she loves me, anyway. Now I can see she's worried, but this time, her commands are no help. I'm still feeling queasy. My head is pounding, and my stomach is lurching.

"Make it stop, Oma," I plead. "I think I'm going to be sick."

"Come and eat something," she urges. "You'll have some tea and rye toast, and that will make you feel better."

Food is the last thing I want, but obediently, I follow Oma into the first class dining room. It is enormous – a grand ballroom lit with pretty chandeliers, each one double or triple my size. There are heavy, red velvet curtains hung across the walls and portholes, held in place with gold braided cords as thick as my waist. Each table is set with white linen tablecloths and matching napkins. There is fancy china, as good as Oma's, and crystal water goblets that sound like musical notes when they are tapped.

The ship's dining rooms were elegantly furnished.

AN BORD DES MOTORSCHIFFES „ST. LOUIS"
Sonntag, den 21. Mai 1939

HAUPTMAHLZEIT

Kaviar auf Röstbrot

Tafelsellerie   Oliven

Minestra
Kraftbrühe mit Markklößchen

Gebratene Seezunge Mirabeau

Lendenschnitte Rossini, Saratoga Chips
Gebratener Mastputer, Selleriefüllung

Stangenspargel, Holländische Tunke
Weinkraut   Spinat in Sahne
Makkaroni in Parmesan
Gekochte, Mus- und Lyoner Kartoffeln

Kopf- und Gurkensalat

Kalifornische Pfirsiche

Suchard-Creme   Eisbecher Carmen
Himbeer-Eis

Holländer und Brie-Käse

Früchte

Kaffee   Tee

Kleine Abendplatten
Roastbeef (kalt), Remoulade, Bratkartoffeln
Corned Beef mit Gemüsesalat
Lammkeule mit Minztunke, Bohnensalat
Schweinskotelett Thomas

Food aboard the *St. Louis* was plentiful and excellent — a welcome treat after the food shortages Jews had faced in Germany. The menu for Sunday dinner on May 21, for instance, featured caviar and California peaches.

I slump down at our table, where Mutti and Phillip are already eating. Mutti sips coffee and Phillip is devouring a bowl of porridge. He looks up and smiles. I think that he is almost pleased to see me ready to vomit.

"Would you like to hear a story I overheard at the hairdressing salon this morning?" Mutti asks. I'm sure she just wants to distract me – to take my mind off my nausea. I stare at my mother, noticing for the first time that her hair is perfectly done. There is even a hair salon on this ship!

"I heard a woman talking," Mutti continues. "She said that two boys had hidden in one of the life boats on board, thinking that it was a game. Their parents were terrified that they might have fallen overboard, and reported it to the captain."

I glance over at Phillip. His face is turned to Mutti's, and his eyes are round as marbles.

"The crew had to search the entire ship before the boys were found. You can imagine the trouble they are in."

"Our children would never to do such a thing!" Oma adds, leveling a long stare at Phillip. But I have had enough of stories. Another wave of nausea sweeps over me.

"My poor Liselotte," says Mutti as I lower my forehead to the table and close my eyes. "It will take a while for you to get used to the waves, but you'll feel better soon. I'm sure of it."

"Is there something I can bring you, Fräulein Freund?" I lift my head and gaze up into the kind eyes of a young waiter who is serving our table. He even knows our family's last name, though I don't think we told him. "I'm so sorry that you're not feeling well. But as your mother says, you'll adjust to the motion of the sea soon enough."

"Just a glass of milk, *bitte*, please," I reply. But the words are barely out of my mouth before I am running for the door of the dining room with Mutti close behind. She has wisely brought a large bowl with her, and I throw up whatever was left of last night's dinner, before slinking off with Mutti to our cabin, and crawling into the dimness of my lower bunk.

Mutti rubs my back, and wipes my forehead with a cool, damp cloth. "You know, my darling, now that we have left Germany, I think it's time to change your name."

Even though I am struggling to keep from vomiting again, I am curious and roll over in my bunk to look at her.

"Nothing drastic, my darling." She smiles as she says this. "But after Cuba, we are going to live in the United Sates once our quota numbers come up, and Liselotte is such a long, German-sounding name. I think, from now on, I will call you Lisa. That sounds more American, don't you think?"

I feel too nauseous to say anything, and roll over again to face the wall. *Lisa*. That's my new American name, and I like the sound of it. I hope that the children I meet in my new country will like it too – that is, if I ever get to the United States.... Mutti said it would take two weeks for this voyage just to reach Cuba. Then I don't know how we will get to America. The way I feel now, I don't know if I can last for two more days, let alone two whole weeks. The waiter said I would get better, but right now, I can't believe it. And even though I am longing to be in America, I'd give anything to get off of this horrid, heaving, tilting boat! All I want is solid ground.

Behind me I can hear that Mutti is tiptoeing out, closing the cabin door softly behind her. After a few moments I pick up my copy of *Madeline* from the small table next to my bunk, thinking maybe I can lose myself for a short time in my storybook. "In an old house in Paris that was covered in vines, lived twelve little girls in two straight lines..." But that's as far as I get. The words are bouncing up and down in front of my eyes, and suddenly my stomach is bouncing as well, and I dive over the side of my bed and bend over the bowl that Mutti has left behind.

Finally, I wipe my mouth with a cool cloth and lie back on my pillow, hugging my beautiful porcelain doll and burying my face in her long braids. "I'm Lisa now," I whisper to her, before sleep floats me away.

SOL

OUR CABIN IS right at sea level, just as Papa said it would be. When I open the porthole, the water is just beneath the window. An ocean wave sprays up and soaks my face, and I laugh out loud. I don't mind the cold water. I love the feel of the sea against my face. I even like the sharp taste of the salt as I lick my lips.

"We won't be able to keep the porthole open all the time," Papa warns. "If the waves become too fierce, we will have to close it. Then you'll have to settle for watching the ocean from the top deck."

We are at sea, and I have woken to bright sunshine beaming in through our small window. Our cabin is tiny, but it's fine for the three of us. My parents share the bottom of the bunk bed, while I sleep on top. There is a small wardrobe for our belongings, and a washroom. What more do we need? I don't care how small our room is as long as we have that porthole, right across from my bed, with golden sunlight and fresh air pouring in. I wouldn't trade that for the biggest, fanciest cabin on the first class deck far above us.

It's time for breakfast, and I drag Mutti and Papa into the third class dining room and find our little table in one corner. The dining room is big and impressive – dark, wooden floors and polished wooden railings to match. The tablecloths are brightly colored, we each have matching cloth napkins, and the plates and bowls even have flowers painted on the rims. The noise in here is deafening. Families are seated at tables of four, six, or ten. Mothers are feeding their infant children, while the fathers devour plates of bread and cheese. A few of the religious men and women are bowing their heads in prayer before and after their meals.

I am starving!

"The sea air makes you hungry," Papa agrees, as the waiter comes over to pour tea into his glass. Papa drops cubes of sugar and a lemon slice into the steaming amber liquid, and then takes a big gulp, even though it is scalding hot. We have not seen so much food in a long time. In the months when Papa was away and money was scarce, there was so little to eat. I often went to bed with a gnawing hollow in my stomach. But here, there is more than enough food for everyone. The waiter places a jug of creamy milk on our table, along with stacks of toast and platters of smoked fish and fresh sliced tomatoes. It is a feast.

"Can we eat it all?" I ask as Papa laughs and nods. Even Mutti has begun to smile. The deep worry lines are fading away from her eyes and mouth. I feel so happy seeing her butter some toast for me and Papa, just like the old days.

The crewmembers are all so kind and polite to us, I can hardly believe it. They address my father by his last name, Herr Messinger. They even call me *"mein Herr,"* or sometimes *"mein junger Herr,"* because I am still a boy. These are German crewmembers, and yet they are so different from the German people we left behind in Berlin. Here, they seem to like us, even though we are Jews.

"The captain, a wonderful man, is setting an example for the crew," Papa says when I ask him why this is. "He respects us when so many Germans don't – even though this is risky to his career."

I know that it is against the law for anyone to help Jews these days.

"If only there were more like him," Mutti adds, and I nod, with my mouth full of buttered toast. I haven't seen the captain yet, but I hope I get to. Maybe I could even thank him for sailing us to Cuba – and for telling his crew to treat us so well.

"What should we do after breakfast?" Papa asks.

"I want to go swimming!" One of the stewards has told me that there is a real swimming pool on this ship. I have never been in one before. In fact, I can't really swim, even though I have waded and paddled in lakes, and in the North Sea.

"Done!" Papa agrees with a hearty laugh.

"I'm not so sure, Zalmon," Mutti says, grabbing Papa by the arm. "Shloimele can't swim and the pool will be deep and perhaps crowded." In an instant, those worry lines have reappeared. But my father brushes her hand and her nervousness aside.

"Nonsense, Pesha," he says. "What harm can come to him if we are standing right there watching? It will be fine. Stop worrying. Let the boy enjoy himself."

So that's what we do. Right after breakfast, I rush back to our

Sol swam in the pool on the sports deck, despite his mother's fear.

cabin with my parents and quickly change into my swimsuit. I grab a towel, and we make our way to the sports deck where the swimming pool is located. There are several families there already. Children are splashing in the water while their parents look on. I drop my towel and wade into the shallow end of the pool.

"Careful, Shloimele," my mother calls. She can't help herself, I know. Her fear comes from the days of seeing me roughed up by tough German children. But right now, I don't want her to watch over me. It reminds me of when she wouldn't let me play in the courtyard of our apartment building. I try to ignore her. And even though I can't swim, I will go as far into the water as I dare. I won't let it go over my head.

The water is cold, but I don't mind that either. I splash around in the shallow end, pretending that I am swimming in the North Sea with my family. I imagine what Edith will say when I tell her I swam in a pool on the *St. Louis*. I doubt she has ever even seen a swimming pool.

"What's your name?" asks a boy floating near me. He looks about my age, though he is a little taller than I am.

"Sol," I say, trying it out. Even though my parents call me Salo and my mother even calls me Shloimele, which is what she has called me since I was a baby, I want to start using the name that I've decided to use in our new lives.

"I'm Leon," he tells me, pushing his dark-rimmed glasses up on his nose. "Maybe we can meet to do some exploring later on."

I nod, we both grin, and he swims away. A friend! It's been such a long time since I had someone to play with. I wave to Mutti and she raises her hand to shield her eyes from the sun. Papa puts his arm around her shoulder, and I can see her face relax.

The ship is picking up speed. Even here in the pool, I can feel the growing swells. But I like it when the waves splash up into my face. If this keeps up, I guess tonight we won't be able to open the porthole.

Sol's family had vacationed on the North Sea – from left are Sol, his father, Aunt Rose, cousin Simi, Uncle Adolf, Sol's mother, cousin Edith, and Aunt Frieda.

WHAT THE CAPTAIN KNEW

WITHIN AN HOUR of leaving the Hamburg port, Captain Schroeder received a telegram from his head office in Germany. It said that two other ships, each one carrying a boatload of Jewish refugees, had left Europe at the same time as the *St. Louis*, and were also heading for Cuba. The wording of the cable disturbed Captain Schroeder. Although it said that no matter what happened, the *St. Louis* passengers would be allowed to land, it advised him to "speed" to Havana. The last sentence of the cable, "No cause for alarm," did alarm the captain. What was going on?

Captain Schroeder wondered why he had not already been told about these two other ships; the *Orduña,* carrying 72 Jewish passengers from Great Britain, and the *Flandre* carrying 104 French Jews. He worried that if there were two other ships en route to Havana, this might interfere with his passengers' ability to land there. Three ships of Jewish refugees might simply be too much for any one country to take in. The wording of the cable was also puzzling. While on the one hand, it assured the captain that his passengers would have no problems landing in Cuba, it also advised him to speed up his journey. Why rush if there were not going to be any problems? The telegram made Captain Schroeder suspect that there might be trouble ahead for his shipload of Jewish passengers.

Two days later, the *St. Louis* made its scheduled stop in Cherbourg, France, to pick up the last 38 of the travelers, thus bringing the total number of refugees on board to 937. In Cherbourg the captain received a second cable from the head office, which urged him again to increase his speed to Havana, and warned of some possible difficulties there.

Two similar warnings within two days. This was more worrying than ever. Though the captain tried to get an explanation of what possible problems were mounting in Cuba, he received no further information. Without any more details, Captain Schroeder believed he had to get out of the Cherbourg harbor as quickly as he could and make all possible speed for Cuba, hoping to beat out the arrival of the two other ships.

Once at sea, he ordered the ship's speed be increased to its maximum, aware that this would make the roll of the vessel worse. He also knew that many of his passengers would then become seasick, but he felt he had no choice. Better to have sick passengers than risk losing the opportunity for his ship to get to Cuba first.

What no one at his head office had told him was that there were mounting protests in Cuba about the possible arrival of Jewish refugees from Europe. These public demonstrations against the refugees were having an effect on the President of Cuba, Federico Laredo Bru. Nobody on board knew that, in the face of these rising protests, President Bru had issued a new ruling canceling all landing permits for the passengers of the *St. Louis*. It was called Decree 937, and the number

The president of Cuba, Federico Laredo Bru

assigned to this law was identical to the number of passengers on board the ship. The landing documents, for which many Jewish families had paid their entire life savings, would be of no use to them.

In addition to signing his Decree 937, President Bru was also in conflict with Manuel Benitez, the Cuban Immigration Director who had taken so much money from the Jews for their landing visas. President Bru knew that Benitez had made a lot of money from the sale of those permits, and he was angry that none of this wealth had been shared with him. When Benitez tried to persuade Bru to reverse his decree canceling the landing permits for the *St. Louis* passengers, Bru dismissed him.

By this time, the United States had learned of the departure of the *St. Louis* from Germany. The U.S. authorities began to fear that many of the passengers who did not have U.S. visas would still try to make their way into America. The U.S., like many other countries, was not eager for this to happen. In 1938, U.S. President Franklin Delano Roosevelt had organized a series of meetings in France. Known as the Evian Conference, it brought together leaders from thirty-one countries including Australia, Brazil, Denmark, Canada, France, Ireland, Sweden, and Great Britain. The purpose of these meetings was to decide what to do with the increasing number of Jews who were trying to escape from Nazi Germany. But when these countries were asked if they would admit some of these refugees, only one of the thirty-one countries would agree to do so. The Dominican Republic offered to accept 100,000 people. No one else wanted Jewish refugees within their borders.

As Captain Schroeder steered the *St. Louis* at top speed toward Cuba, Jewish representatives from the United States were arriving on the island to try to help resolve what they sensed might be a bad situation. Among these was Morris Troper, the European Director of the American Jewish Joint Distribution Committee (JDC), an organization focused on helping Jews escape Nazi Europe. In meetings with Cuban officials, and with representatives of the Hamburg-American Line, Troper was repeatedly reassured that the Jews of the *St. Louis* would be able to land in Cuba.

From the very beginning, Troper had trouble believing this.

Lisa

I TRIED going for a walk on the deck with Mutti. I even took one of my dolls with me, thinking it would make me feel better to hold on to her as I took some wobbly steps outside my cabin. As soon as we got outside, Mutti and I sank down onto two of the long chairs that are lined up side by side, facing the ocean. These chairs have soft cushions that make them feel as cozy as my bed at home.

"I think I'm alright for now, Mutti," I said cautiously. I lay back and stared out at the sea in front of me. My mother didn't answer. She lay still with her eyes closed. I don't think Mutti is feeling well out here! I pulled my doll closer, wrapping my sweater around her to protect her from the cool wind that blew across the ship's decks. Oma says that it will start to get warmer as we get closer to Cuba.

There are so many people walking back and forth in front of me. There's even a man on roller skates! He raises one leg behind him as he glides by, lifting his cap as if to greet me. He looks so funny. I shake Mutti's arm to make her look, and she smiles weakly. The other passengers move aside as he zigzags through the crowd. Everyone is staring at him as if he is a performer in a circus show. He is being chased by some children who look to be my age. I wish I could go and play with

A man who roller-skated on the sports deck fascinated passengers.

them. I wish I could put on skates and weave my way across the ship. But I barely trust myself to stand up at this point. Maybe soon I'll play shuffleboard, or go swimming, or even roller-skate. If only my head would stop spinning!

The truth is, I'm still seasick. Aside from that one walk on the deck with Mutti, I haven't left my dark bottom bunk in days. I lie here, curled in a ball, praying for the heaving motion to stop and my dizziness and lurching stomach to settle down. Mutti says the ship is going faster than it did at the beginning. That's why there's so much tilting and rocking. The ship is bouncing against the waves that are crashing up to meet it. But while slowing down might make the trip smoother, to my mind, we can't get to Cuba fast enough. I wish I could fly across this endless ocean – anything to get me onto solid land.

I have no idea what Phillip does all the time. He comes back to our cabin at the end of the day and climbs into the bunk above me without a word. That part is normal; he rarely talks to me at the best of times. But I wonder what he's been up to. I wonder if he has made friends with anyone on the ship, and if he is enjoying himself exploring the decks and doing everything that I am not able to do.

Just like me, Mutti is also sick and has taken to her bed. In the beginning, she said the rocking didn't bother her much. But several days later, she too began to look pale. Now she can't move, and Oma is running between my bed and Mutti's, taking care of both of us.

"Come, Liselotte, you must try to sip a bit of plain broth that I have brought you. You'll waste away to nothing if you don't try to eat a little." Oma has not yet learned to call me Lisa. Perhaps she never will. Grandmothers are like that, I think – set in their ways. She strokes my hair and holds my head up so that I can sip the warm liquid. It is good, I must admit. But after one or two sips, I feel sick again. I push the soup bowl away and lie back down on my pillow, biting my lip hard to keep from throwing up.

"There, there, child," soothes Oma. "We'll try again later."

This is the gentlest I've seen my grandmother in a long time. And even though my head is pounding, I love this time with her and don't want her to leave. "What will America be like, Oma?" I ask, trying to keep her there talking to me despite my queasiness.

"We'll see your Aunt Edith and Uncle Werner," she replies, "along with your cousin, Arthur. It will be good to be with family again, won't it?"

I nod, but don't say anything. My mother's twin sister, Edith, and her husband, my Uncle Werner, managed to get out of Germany with their son months before we did. Uncle Werner is a doctor. Oma brushes my hair back from my forehead and tells me he has done some very important work – something to do with skin diseases. She says that the American government probably agreed to admit Uncle Werner and his family, even though they are Jews, because they saw how valuable his skills might be.

"It was difficult for him at first because he was there in New York alone," Oma explained. "From there, he traveled to a small city called Hackensack."

It's such a funny name and even now, sick as I feel, I can't help but laugh when I hear it.

"When he found a place in Hackensack, Uncle Werner sent for your aunt and your cousin," Oma continued. "There are so many people here on the ship who have no one waiting for them. We're very lucky to have family already in America. They have sponsored us, and in addition to our entry permits into Cuba, we also have visas to America. Cuba will be just a short stop for us.

"And you'll go to school in America, Liselotte," my grandmother continues. "Won't that be wonderful?"

I nod again. That's the part that I can hardly wait for. I love the thought of an American school. I can't wait to sit in a classroom where I will learn English and read as many books as I want!

I feel a bit less nauseous when I think about happier days. I decide that I might try to get up and go for a short walk on the deck.

"I'm sure the fresh sea air will be good for you, my child," Oma says. "Come. And if you're feeling well enough, I will take you to the cinema. There is a film showing this evening. Your mother has no desire to go, but perhaps you and I will."

The cinema! At this I brighten even more. I love the movies I used to see in Munich – before the theaters were banned to Jews. I sit up in my bunk and slowly swing my legs to the floor. I can hardly stand up on my own. My steps are so weak and shaky, I feel like I'm a baby learning to walk. Oma grabs me under the arms to help steady me.

"There's nothing left of you, my child," she gasps. "You must start eating again."

My skirt does feel loose around my waist, but there's nothing I can do about that. I walk past Mutti, who is lying down. She raises a weak hand to pat my cheek. Her face is as white as the sheet that she pulls up to cover herself. Then, Oma and I step outside.

It is raining and a fine mist sprays against my face, blown by a sweep of cool air. I grasp tightly on to Oma's arm, taking deep breaths to keep from gagging.

"I'm right here," Oma says reassuringly. "Just keep walking, I'm right beside you."

"*Guten Abend*. Good evening, little Fräulein." A steward passes and smiles at me. "I understand you've not been well."

I don't trust myself to speak. So instead, I just try to return the smile.

"Well, if it's any consolation, you're not alone. Many passengers have been seasick. The ship is going at full speed. The captain doesn't want to waste any time getting to Cuba." He looks up at my grandmother. "We do have a doctor on board – Doctor Walter Glauner – if you need any help for your family."

"*Danke*. Thank you," my grandmother replies. "But we are doing just fine. I'm taking my granddaughter to the cinema this evening."

"Wonderful idea. It's a romantic film tonight. Should be just the ticket to make her feel better. *Gute Nacht*. Goodnight, Fräulein."

"Gute Nacht, mein Herr," I manage.

Once inside the theater, I sink into a seat. There are many families in the audience, and the room is noisy. Children are running up and down the aisles while their parents beg them to sit and be still. Some men and women in the row ahead of us are chatting about how the journey has gone so far.

"This morning the ship passed so close to the Azores that I could actually see the windmills on shore," one man exclaims, and goes on to tell his friends that these islands, right in the middle of the Atlantic, are volcanic.

A lady nods at him, "We must be half way to Cuba – or more – by now."

I try to shut out the noise around me and close my eyes. I'm determined to stay for the movie. I can't let this whole voyage go by in my bunk!

The lights dim and the screen lights up. As we all wait, looking forward to the film, a newsreel begins, and the angry face of Adolf Hitler fills the screen. He is making a speech about "evil" Jews to a crowd of thousands who have gathered to cheer and support him. He screams that rich Jews are plotting together all over the world to push Germany into war. And if the Jews don't stop, he says, they will be completely erased from Europe!

There are hundreds of German tanks passing the podium where Hitler stands, and platoons of soldiers are marching by, saluting him with outstretched arms, while the crowds chant like never-ending thunder, "*Sieg Heil.* Hail to victory!"

Hitler is so huge on the screen that I can even see his eyebrows twitch and droplets of spit fly from his mouth. There is a line of perspiration across his forehead that he wipes with a white handkerchief. Gasps fill the theater, and then there is silence. A moment later, the newsreel is finished and the film begins. But I have had enough. The sight of Hitler screaming hate has turned my stomach. I run from the theater with Oma at my heels. She is boiling over with anger, and ranting against the crew of the ship. "How could they possibly have allowed such a disgusting piece of film to be shown to us? Have they no sensitivity? I'll find out who is responsible for this and trust me, it will not happen again!"

I barely hear a word that she's saying. I'm still shocked by the sight of Hitler on the screen – so big and terrifying that the image feels burned into my brain. I remember again why we are fleeing our home. I know even more surely that we Jews are in terrible danger. I need to get to the safety of my bed and close my eyes and my mind. I am feeling so sick that I barely make it to our cabin. I can't tell if this flood of nausea is from the ship's movement, or from the newsreel which plays over and over in my head.

I use the big bowl again.

SOL

I HAVE DISCOVERED that Leon, the boy I met in the swimming pool, is staying in the cabin diagonally across from mine! We have spent the last few days exploring the whole ship together. We are roaming every single deck to see what there is to see. And each day brings a new discovery.

The sports deck holds not only that great swimming pool, there is also a shuffleboard court there, and a gymnasium, too. I have never played shuffleboard before, and neither Leon nor I are very good at it. But that doesn't stop us from picking up the cues and sliding the disks across the slippery floor at top speed. The ship has a nightclub on Deck B called the *Tanzplatz*. I haven't been there at night; it's mostly for grown-ups. But it is a really fancy ballroom, lit by rows of crystal chandeliers, and lined with big, shiny mirrors in heavy, gold frames.

It is amazing what you can discover when you explore all the

Adults and children lined up to play shuffleboard on the sports deck.

different decks. Sometimes a girl tags along with me and Leon. She's about my age, has curly, black hair, and a wide smile. I always forget her name, probably because she's a girl. Since she has no trouble keeping up, she follows us around, and we don't really mind.

The ship is still traveling very fast, and I love the speed and the big waves. At the beginning of our trip we started with small swells, but now they are powerful white-water breakers, crashing against the hull with so much force that the spray comes up as high as Deck 5. As we walk the decks we can feel the ship heaving, moving from side to side, and up and down. We have to hold on to the railing to keep from falling. The ship is moving in a zigzag course, trying to avoid some of the bigger swells. But that only works for a short period before the rocking begins again. In the dining rooms, the stewards have raised the sides of the tables so that plates of food do not slide off, and onto the floor. One of the stewards told me they do this whenever there is a storm at sea. I guess they are set up for anything on this big ship.

Many people on board have become seasick, but not me. I eat lots and lots in the half-empty dining room. And the rolling decks don't stop me, Leon, and the girl with the curly, black hair from having our adventures, either. There are folding deck chairs on every level, and the most fun we have is bouncing on the chairs, using them like trampolines. I don't think the grown-ups like our game. Some of them frown at us as we dodge around them and jump on every empty chair. Sometimes they yell and shake their fingers at us too, but that doesn't really make us stop. I'm not even sure that Mutti and Papa would approve if they knew what we were doing. But Papa has finally convinced Mutti to let me explore on my own. She was reluctant at first, but has released me from under her watchful eyes.

Every now and then I catch a glimpse of the Nazi flag flying from the rear of the ship. I had hoped I'd never have to look at it again, and I wonder why the captain doesn't take it down. Even Papa doesn't know the answer to that question when I ask him. But Leon and I try not to play anywhere near the flag so we don't have to see it.

I feel so free on this ship. I haven't had a chance to play without Mutti watching in such a long time. I shout to my friends to follow me, and they jump in line behind me. This is what freedom feels like – my fears just fall away from me like so many layers of heavy clothing. It's as if we have flown off the earth and landed on a magical, new planet. I meet Leon and the girl with the curly, black hair at the same place, every day. I can't wait to get to Cuba, which can only be better.

In between exploring with my friends, I keep my parents company. The three of us stroll the decks together, talking eagerly about where we will live, where I will go to school, and the new friends that I will meet in Cuba. I haven't had family time with my parents – just the three of us – in so long. My mother links her arm with my father's, and I hold his hand on the other side. Sometimes we don't have to say anything at all. It is enough just to be walking together.

RIGHT: Sol and his mother, standing near the center of the photo, mingled with other passengers on the deck.

Three of the big halls on board the ship are also used as synagogues. It is *Shavuot*, a very important Jewish holiday that celebrates the day that Moses and the Israelites received the Torah and God's commandments at Mount Sinai. This holiday comes after Passover, when we celebrate the day that Jews were granted their freedom from slavery. Today I'm going to services with my Papa. This reminds me of when we used to go to the synagogue together, hand in hand in Berlin, before Papa was taken away and the synagogue was burnt to the ground. Here on the ship, we can pray safely and openly. It's like we have been freed from slavery, too!

"Will we go to synagogue in Cuba, Papa?" I ask.

"Of course." My father smiles and pulls me along so that we can get to the service on time. It is raining today, and the wind has picked up speed, along with the ship. I pull my cap down over my forehead and the collar of my jacket up to my ears as I run to keep pace with my father. "I'm sure that Edith and your Aunt Frieda and Uncle Adolf have already found a synagogue for our families to attend."

"And will there be parks for us to walk to after services?"

Papa nods again. "And, Salo, dearest son, none of them will have yellow benches where Jews are forced to sit apart from others." He stops and pulls me close to him when he says this, staring deeply into my eyes. Then he takes a deep breath and we continue walking.

I am enjoying this moment with my Papa, so much so that I barely notice the commotion up ahead. Several families are leaving the hall even before the services have begun. One man marches past us, his face almost purple with rage.

"An insult!" he shouts to no one in particular. "I'm going straight to the captain to complain about this."

"What is it?" Papa stops another man who is also leaving the hall.

The man barely pauses. "During the night, someone hung a picture of Adolf Hitler in the hall," he finally says. "It was there to greet us when we arrived for services this morning. I left Germany to get away from that madman," he adds. "Is he to follow us all the way to Cuba?"

This man also looks as if he is ready to explode with anger. He storms off followed by others, all of whom seem to have given up on the Shavuot services.

"Papa?" I ask. An old, familiar dread is creeping across my neck and raising the hairs on my scalp. Who could have done this? It obviously wasn't a passenger. But I can't imagine that it could possibly have been a member of the crew. They all seem so kind, from the waiters in the dining room to the stewards who allow me and Leon and the girl with the curly, black hair to run up and down the decks. But maybe there are crewmembers who do secretly hate Jews, and this is their way of showing it – showing us that we are not free yet. Maybe that's why the Nazi flag is still here, flying from the back of the ship.

"Perhaps not everyone on board has the same good intentions," Papa replies, as if he is reading my thoughts. I suddenly feel exactly like I did years ago on the day the park benches were painted yellow.

There are people who hate and despise us. Drops of rain are sliding down my face and the ship is tilting side to side beneath my feet, but I barely notice. Papa takes my hand again, but this time he pulls me away from the hall. We will not go to the services, either. We turn and leave this deck, and make our way to our cabin at the bottom of the ship. We walk silently, my Papa and me. Tomorrow I will meet my friends again, and we will roam the ship and play games together, and I will try to forget this. But like memories of the times we left behind in Berlin, these moments are giving me goose bumps, and I can feel my hands are sweaty despite the cold. I wonder if hatred will follow us no matter where we go.

Sol and his parents pose on the deck of the *St. Louis*.

WHAT THE CAPTAIN KNEW

THERE WERE MANY crewmembers on board the *St. Louis* who, like Captain Gustav Schroeder, did not agree with the Nazi Party's belief that Jews were an inferior race, to be despised and harmed. Klaus Ostermeyer, the ship's first officer and Ferdinand Mueller, a purser, were two of the officers who admired Captain Schroeder and followed his example. They, and many others, were determined to treat the Jewish passengers with kindness and respect, as the captain had ordered.

However, the captain was sure that there were other crewmembers who were not so eager to be good to the Jewish families. The worst of these was a man named Otto Shiendick who was on board as a steward, but who was really a spy for the Gestapo – the much-feared secret police of the Nazis. He was there to make the guests uncomfortable, to search out any crewmembers who did not support the Nazi Party, and to keep an eye on the captain. He did his job well, going so far as to play a newsreel featuring Adolf Hitler in the ship's cinema, and hanging a picture of Hitler in one of the social halls. He also gathered supportive crewmembers in the Tanzplatz to sing Nazi victory songs. Captain Schroeder had forbidden these kinds of activities. He knew that any reminder of Hitler would be an insult to his Jewish passengers, and would frighten those who had already experienced acts of anti-Semitism in their former homeland. But it was difficult even for the captain to control all the actions of every member of his crew at all times. And since Shiendick was from the Gestapo, there was only so much that the captain could do to stop this representative of the ruling party. He could not, for example, lower the swastika flag that flew at the back of the ship. This was an order straight from the Gestapo.

Otto Shiendick had one more reason for being on board the *St. Louis*. He was traveling to meet another Nazi spy in Havana. Once in Cuba, Shiendick would be meeting with this spy to pick up blueprints for U.S. submarines and destroyers, which he was supposed to take back to the Gestapo in Germany. This plan had a code name – Operation Sunshine – and the Nazi spy in Havana was Robert Hoffman, the assistant manager of the Havana office of the shipping line that owned the *St. Louis*.

Ironically, even though Shiendick did not care about what happened to the Jewish passengers on board, it was extremely important to him to have the ship land in Havana, so that he could carry out his Gestapo orders, and meet with Hoffman.

But as Captain Schroeder piloted his ship at top speed through the Atlantic, things in Havana were getting more and more complicated. Even after the Cuban president had passed Decree 937, canceling the landing permits for the Jews on board, Manuel Benitez, the Immigration Officer who had issued those permits, was continuing to reassure everyone from the shipping company that the passengers would be allowed to land. He said that the permits he had issued had been signed before Decree 937 had been passed – therefore they had to be valid and legal.

Benitez had never hidden the fact that he had made a lot of money from the sale of those landing documents. At the same time, he proclaimed himself to be a good friend and ally of the Jews, working on their behalf. When it came right down to it, he was really interested only in his own welfare. He did not want to clash with President Bru, so he searched for a way to get around the president's latest decree without a direct confrontation. Benitez was an arrogant, overly confident man who believed that Bru would eventually back down and allow the ship's passengers to disembark – particularly if the *St. Louis* was already in the Havana harbor. He was also convinced that at some point he would be able to offer Bru a bribe, either a share of his own profits, or money that the shipping company would pay, in order to slip the 937 passengers into Havana.

In the midst of all of this, the Americans in Cuba who were there to work on behalf of the Jewish refugees were also running into obstacles. In addition to Morris Troper, the Director of the American Jewish Joint Committee, there was another America-based organization in Havana, the Jewish Relief Committee, dedicated to helping refugees who had already escaped Germany, and those who were still coming out, including the passengers of the *St. Louis*. But they did not have a lot of money, and though they had asked for funds from the government of the United States, nothing had arrived. They needed money to try to combat the anti-Semitic newspaper reports that were being published in Havana on an almost daily basis. And every day they were receiving inquiries from Jewish families already in Cuba who had relatives on board the *St. Louis*. The committee continually reassured these families that their relatives would be fine and would soon be joining them, but in fact, they were starting to feel hopeless about this possibility. They were also more and more concerned that the United States might not help the refugees, if asked.

Back on board the *St. Louis*, Captain Schroeder shared none of his own worries about the fate of his ship and its passengers. His concern was to get the ship to Cuba as quickly as possible, with everyone safe and healthy. This was not to be. On board was an elderly couple, Recha and Moritz Weiler. Though Recha was relieved to be sailing toward freedom, Moritz, a retired university professor, was less positive about their future. And he was not well physically. The depression and poor health that he had suffered for some time only deepened once the ship set sail. On Tuesday, May 23, Moritz passed away on board the *St. Louis*. The captain had no choice but to bury him at sea. In order not to frighten or disturb the other passengers, Captain Schroeder arranged for a rabbi to perform the service at 11:00 p.m. when he believed that most on board would be sleeping. The captain later wrote in his own personal diary these thoughts about Moritz:

> *It broke his heart to feel that in his old age, he had to leave the land where, all his life long, he had worked on the best of terms with his colleagues … one felt that his will to live had gone.*[2]

Shortly after the burial, a crewmember, depressed over these events, jumped overboard from the same spot that Moritz Weiler's body had been slipped into the ocean. He was Leonid Berg, a thirty-year-old kitchen hand. Captain Schroeder ordered the ship to turn around and search for the missing man, knowing that this would cost them precious time in getting to Cuba. The missing crewmember was never found, and after several hours, the ship continued on its journey.

Lisa

WE ARE GETTING closer to Havana. It's not that anyone has actually told me this. But today around noon I decided I would get up again, and try to walk to the dining room for something to eat. I have hardly left my cabin since that time I went to the cinema with my Oma – the outing that ended so badly with the enormous face of Adolf Hitler raging on the screen in front of me.

I have not talked about that horrible night with anyone – not with Oma, not with Mutti, and certainly not with Phillip, who continues to disappear from our room each morning and then reappear just as mysteriously at the end of each day. From the little that Phillip says to me, I have learned that, since Mutti allows him to roam the ship unsupervised, he has made friends with a few other boys on board. It seems there are endless places to discover on this ship and he is having the time of his life. He goes to the games deck and plays shuffleboard.

He has even gone to the cinema without Mutti and Oma, though I don't think he saw the same scary newsreel that we saw. Oma had one short conversation with Mutti about the incident when we got back to the cabin that night. Actually, it wasn't really a conversation, because Mutti was too seasick to respond. But Oma ranted on, anyway.

"Disgraceful!" she kept repeating. "The captain will hear from me. In fact, once I've put Liselotte to bed, I'm marching over to his cabin to make a formal complaint. He must know how this parading of Hitler has offended me and many others."

I don't know if Oma ever really complained to the captain. I don't know if he did anything about the newsreel, or if he even found the horrible person who had played this cruel trick on us. Oma has said nothing about it since then, and I have crept back into my bunk to spend these last days alone, still seasick. I'm dreaming of getting off the ship and onto a surface that doesn't roll up and down and make my stomach do the same!

Can you imagine? We've been sailing for two weeks now and I have only gotten out of bed a couple of times. It's as if I have lost two whole weeks of my life! Well, no more. Today, I am getting up and I am going to stay up.

I am weaker than I thought I would be, but of course I've hardly eaten anything in days. My head feels dizzy when I stand up. But Mutti curves her arm tight around my shoulders and guides me along. Pretty soon, we are helping each other to walk, because this is the first time in days that Mutti has left her sick bed, too. Oma is quite exhausted from nursing both of us, though she would never complain about that, or about anything, for that matter. Oma is too proud to ever complain. But today, Mutti and I are giving Oma a much-needed break. We head out of our cabin, "two recovering invalids," Mutti jokes, and take wobbly steps onto the deck.

It is Friday, May 26. I know this because Mutti has been keeping track of the days for us, counting them down the same way I used to count down the hours until my birthdays. As we step out onto the deck I can feel a change in the mood of the passengers, just like you can feel a change in the weather. They seem eager, somehow. And the weather is different, too! The sea air is warmer – I can feel a soft breeze carrying damp heat across the deck.

Suddenly, people are pushing by Mutti and me, nearly knocking us off our feet in their rush to get to the railing. There is a boy, older than me, who is bouncing up and down on the deck chairs, with other children who are following his lead. They stop and run to the railing, too. Even the religious men and women, who usually look so serious, are smiling and nodding to everyone as they speed across the deck. We join the passengers at the railing, staring out at the horizon. I can see a distant, green shoreline. I can make out buildings! And trees that look like palm trees, even though I've never seen one in real life. I recognize them from books that I have read.

I pull Mutti closer, pointing to the distance. "What is that?" I'm practically breathless.

Mutti shakes her head, unsure, and then stops a passing steward. He follows Mutti's pointing finger and smiles at us. "It's Miami, Fräulein – the coast of Florida in the United States. We should be arriving in Cuba tomorrow." Then he wrinkles his brow, touches his cap, bows slightly, and rushes off muttering, "So much to do to get ready! So much to do…." It's as if he too has suddenly realized how close we are to the end of our journey. We are so close that I can actually see land – right over there is American land!

"We're still a whole day away," Mutti says, smiling at my rising excitement and putting her arm around me again. "Soon the ship will leave this coastline and sail on to Cuba. But one day soon, Lisa, we will be back here in America," she adds. "And not just watching it from a ship. We will be living here."

All at once, I am not feeling sick. It is amazing what hope can do. It can erase the worst feelings, and make you feel so much better.

Mutti and I, suddenly famished, make our way to the dining room. The big room is nearly empty. Most of the first class passengers have already had their lunch, including Oma and Phillip, who are nowhere to be seen. Only a few couples are left at their tables, sipping tea and coffee, and listening to the small orchestra that is serenading the passengers as they eat. I don't recognize this music. It's not the classical music and opera that I know best, from the records Oma plays on her phonograph. Mutti tells me that these are modern American songs. "Glenn Miller," she says, humming the melody under her breath. "He is a famous American composer and band leader." The music is fast, and has a beat that makes me want to dance. I love this music, and I hope that I will hear more songs like this when we are finally ashore.

"Will the young Miss be attending the costume ball this evening?" A waiter has approached our table and is placing a bowl of clear soup with dumplings in front of me. The smell is heavenly.

"A costume ball?"

"Of course," he replies. "It's a tradition on the last night of the voyage."

I look at Mutti, hoping that she is as excited about this news as I am. But she shakes her head. "We must pack up our things this evening. And my daughter has not been well. She needs her sleep," Mutti says. "I'm sure there will be lovely costume parties in America," she adds, seeing the instant disappointment in my eyes, and reaching out to touch my face. "We'll be in Cuba tomorrow, Lisa. Don't you want to be fresh and wide awake when you walk off the ship?"

I nod hesitantly. Of course I want to be ready. In fact, I'd like to be the first one off the ship, though I doubt that will be possible! Still, a costume ball sounds like such fun. I wonder if the band will play Glenn Miller melodies for everyone to dance to.

I won't let myself feel bad about this. Mutti is right. There is a lot to do. We must fill our empty suitcases again with all the clothes that we unpacked while we were at sea. And Mutti will help us choose the special outfits that we will wear for our arrival in Cuba. We will lay these out on our beds, waiting for the early morning horn that will wake us to a brand new life. Before I go to sleep I will prepare my dolls, and dress them up in the nice clothes that they, too, will wear to get off the ship. I wonder if I will sleep at all tonight. My head is whirling with visions of palm trees, and white buildings, and new friends and adventures that await me. If I fall asleep, I'll bet my dreams will be more exciting than any ball could ever be.

Many young children sailed with their families on the *St. Louis*.

SOL

THE HORN ANNOUNCING our arrival in Cuba sounded at 4:30 this morning. But I didn't need the loud blasts to wake me. I could not sleep more than a few minutes last night, I was so jumpy. As I tossed and turned in my bunk, I could hear the distant sound of the orchestra playing dance tunes at the costume ball in the grand ballroom. I didn't want to go, and there was no discussion with my parents about whether or not we would attend. Dances are for girls, so why would I want to be there? But before going to bed, I peeked into the ballroom and saw bright, colored streamers and big bunches of balloons hanging from the glittering chandeliers. Though I was in bed pretty early, I was still awake long after the music had faded away. You would think I would be worn out this morning. But as soon as the horn blared out its message that we were in Cuba, I jumped out of my top bunk and begged my parents to get up quickly, too.

It took us no time at all to pack our three small suitcases. Today I am wearing the same trousers and shirt I wore when I boarded the *St. Louis* two weeks ago – they're the only good clothes that I have, really. As we sit in our cabin waiting for our landing instructions, Papa takes out our documents and carefully lays them across the lower bunk. He examines them, delicately turning all the pages, with the closest attention.

"Here are our passports, one for your mother and one for me. You see, Salo, your name is here in your mother's passport."

Our passports don't have the letter "J" stamped on them like Aunt Rose's did. Maybe it's because Papa's set of papers came from Poland. Polish passports were not branded in the same way as German ones.

"And these are our landing permits for Cuba." Papa continues, as he thumbs through the next set of documents. "We paid dearly for these, Salo, but it is worth everything we have to know these will allow us to enter Havana."

"We'll have to watch our money carefully in Cuba," Mutti adds. "One of the rules is that Papa will not be allowed to work while we are here. The Cubans don't want anyone taking their jobs. When we go to the United States, we will be able to work and earn money."

I nod. I don't need anything but some friends and my family. I am used to going without extras. That doesn't bother me one bit.

"And this!" Papa holds up the last of our papers. "This is the permit that will allow us to enter the United States after we have

Passengers on the *St. Louis* were excited to see
the shoreline of Havana after two weeks at sea.

been in Havana for a while. You see this number here, Salo? When this number is called, that's when we will be able to go to America."

"Why do we have to wait? Why can't we go straight there now?" I ask.

Papa's gaze lingers for a moment on the document in his hands, as if he is admiring a precious diamond, and then he looks at me. "There are many Jews like us who are trying to get into America. The government says we must wait our turn."

"It's almost like lining up – the way you used to line up to go to the cinema in Berlin," Mutti explains.

"But we will be patient, and soon our number will come up, and we will go," Papa concludes triumphantly. "And then I'll work again – as a tailor, just the way I used to." I can wait for America, of course. We will all have to wait.

I nearly forgot something wonderful! I will see my cousin Edith again, in Havana – today. All of a sudden my heart swells with happiness.

I open the porthole of our cabin and stare out at the shoreline, which is just beginning to light up. It is still quite dark, with a blue haze against the gray sky and a hint of light about to explode into dawn. The heat of the coming day is already blasting through the opening. The hot wind reminds me of the feeling I once had when I was feverish with diphtheria, a scary infection that can damage your heart. It was just after Aunt Rose had left for Cuba. So not only was

Mutti worrying about Papa, who was in Poland, she was sad over Aunt Rose's departure, *and* she was scared I might die! It took weeks till I got better. My throat swelled up so much that I couldn't swallow, and I could barely breathe. I was burning up – I could feel the scorching heat of my fever rising from my body in waves. The heat of this day does not feel as hot as that fever, nothing could…still, this steamy breeze feels strange on my skin. Mutti says I will get used to everything about Cuba soon enough.

The ship has anchored, but we are not at the pier. We are some distance away from land, in a channel leading up to the port of Havana. I don't know why the ship has not pulled up to the dock, and when I ask Mutti and Papa they shrug their shoulders and shake their heads. Later, as I walk out onto an upper deck, I can overhear passengers asking crewmembers why we are stopped here. The crew does not seem to have much information, either. Each steward or waiter has a different answer.

"Documents must be checked here at sea before the ship can land."

"Health officials will need to board the ship and check that all the passengers are free of infections. Cuba wouldn't want any diseases to reach its shores."

"It's a busy harbor and this is a big ship. They will need to clear a place for us at the dock and this will take some time."

On and on the reasons go. Each makes sense, though it's strange that no one seems to know the real reason, or at least, no one can agree on one. But I'm not worried, and no one else seems very concerned about the delay. Maybe this is what always happens when an ocean liner arrives in a new port. The crewmembers go about their duties and continue to smile and serve the passengers. And the people on board are excited. Women are rushing from their cabins with their children, dressed in their best, leaning on the railings, pointing to sights on the shoreline. Their husbands are carrying bags and boxes that are beginning to line the various decks, just as they once lined the Hamburg pier before our departure. I spot Leon standing with his parents next to the railing, and I catch his eye and wave. He points to the deck chairs nearby and jumps up and down, reminding me that we should have one last adventure on the ship before we get off.

Mutti has come to stand next to me at the railing. "Look," she says, pointing to the shore. "The buildings are pure white. Aren't they beautiful, Shloimele, so clean looking?"

I nod. As the sun rises on the horizon, it catches the white buildings and reflects so brightly that even here at this distance, I have to shield my eyes or be blinded by the glare. Here and there I can spot church steeples that jut up into the sky. What looks like a fortress stands at one end of the harbor, with towering brick walls that rise from the sea. I glance over at Mutti, who seems as captivated by the sights of Havana as I am. Her face is peaceful, and I too feel a quiet joy to be here, leaning against her. Time almost stands still.

"May twenty-seventh," she says, with a special note in her voice. "I will always remember this day."

"Mutti!" I shout, turning away from the railing to face her. "It's your birthday today. How could we forget?"

Mutti looks at me and smiles. "There's no need for a gift or a party, my darling. It's celebration enough just to know that we are finally here."

I can't believe that I have forgotten my mother's birthday. The thought of arriving in Cuba has pushed everything else right out of my mind. We should have a big party for her when we are with Edith and her parents. Yes, that's what we will do, I'll make sure. I hang on to Mutti's arm and daydream of our lives in this new white city.

WHAT THE CAPTAIN KNEW

DAYS BEFORE the *St. Louis* arrived in Havana harbor, Captain Schroeder was already aware that his boatload of Jewish refugees would not be allowed to land. He had received another cable from his head office telling him about the new Decree 937, which meant most of his passengers would be denied entry into Cuba. He was told to speed on, since the situation was not clear, but the cable warned him things could become critical.

The captain was deeply concerned about this message, but because he did not want to alarm his passengers he did not tell them this news. He hoped that this would just be a temporary setback and that, eventually, the ship would be able to dock. He was relieved that the *St. Louis* was arriving in Havana ahead of the two other ships that were also sailing there. The speed with which he had driven his ship had paid off, and at least the *St. Louis* was first in line.

But as the ship approached the harbor, a second cable arrived, telling Captain Schroeder to drop anchor outside the harbor, and warning him not to try to dock the ship. This only added to the anxiety that Captain Schroeder was already feeling. He believed that the passengers on the *St. Louis* were his responsibility until they were on shore and the captain was feeling the increasing weight of the possibility that this might not happen.

Meanwhile, in Havana, hundreds of telegrams were arriving at President Bru's office, urging him to keep the Jewish travelers out of Cuba. The misleading propaganda information being spread by the Nazis was having its desired effect. President Bru was even more convinced that he had been right in passing his Decree 937 to keep the Jews out. Even though Immigration Minister Manuel Benitez tried to see President Bru, he was turned away. Benitez, who had once been a close friend and advisor to the president, could not even get in the door of the presidential palace. Cuba would not be a welcoming place for the Jews on board the *St. Louis*.

The American representatives of the Jewish Relief Committee were desperate for help. Their pleas were finally answered when two people from a New York-based organization arrived in Cuba to take charge of the situation. One was a social worker whose job was to find housing and schools for the passengers on the *St. Louis* if they were given permission to disembark. The other, Lawrence Berenson, was a lawyer who was there to negotiate with President Bru. He offered the president up to $125,000 or the equivalent of almost $2 million in today's dollars, as a guarantee that none of the passengers would ever need financial support from the government of Cuba if they were allowed in the country. Furthermore, he promised that the Jewish passengers would not take jobs away from Cubans by trying to find employment while they were in the country. Berenson hoped that this would be enough to make President Bru back down and allow the passengers of the *St. Louis* to disembark.

Lisa

WE'VE BEEN sitting still for days now, and nothing is happening. Every single passenger is waiting for the captain to announce that the ship will dock shortly, so we can finally get off. But where is that announcement? The captain has not appeared, and no one seems to know why.

"Patience," Mutti says. "We must be patient, and eventually we will land."

Well, I am losing my patience. And even though my stomach is feeling better now that the ship has come to a dead stop, I am still desperate for my feet to finally touch solid ground.

On the first day we stopped here, one of the crew raised a yellow flag at the back of the ship. Another passenger told Mutti it was a "quarantine" flag. That meant we might have diseases on board that would need to be checked. A Cuban doctor from shore sailed out in a small boat and boarded the ship, climbing up a long, narrow ladder that had been lowered to sea level. All of the passengers were told to come to the social hall so that he could examine us for any illnesses.

"Mutti, I've been sick on the trip," I said, a little scared. "Does that mean I won't be able to get off?" We were standing in a long line of passengers that snaked its way around the top deck and into the social hall.

Mutti wrapped her arm around my shoulder. "Please don't worry, Lisa. The doctor is looking for other illnesses, the kind that could spread to people in Havana. A little seasickness will not be one of those."

Still, I stayed close to Mutti, hiding slightly behind her, hoping not to be noticed as our family approached the doctor standing at the front of the line. He wore a white suit, almost as bright as the white buildings I had seen dotting the shoreline of Havana harbor. Doctor Glauner, the ship's doctor, was standing next to him, looking slightly annoyed that someone else had come on board to examine *his* passengers. When we got to the head of the line I held my breath, but the doctor from Havana barely looked at me. He asked Mutti a few questions, which I didn't even hear. The fear of being kept out of Cuba pounded so loudly in my head that it blocked out their voices. Finally, the doctor scribbled something on a sheet of paper, and dismissed Mutti, Oma, Phillip, and me with a quick bow from the waist. I let out my breath in relief. Several hours later, after everyone on board had been examined, the Cuban doctor climbed back down the narrow ladder to his small motorboat, and it roared away from the ship. The yellow flag was lowered.

That was three days ago and we are still here, waiting.

Over the last day or so, little boats have begun to appear around the *St. Louis*. People in sailboats, motorboats, and small dinghies have come out to see the ship and to see the passengers who are on board. Mutti says we are a spectacle to the Havana citizens that have come to gawk at us. I wonder if the people in these small boats know that we are Jews escaping from Germany. I wonder if they realize how much we need to find safety in their country. There – a girl in a small fishing boat is waving to me. I raise my hand and wave back. She looks about my age. Her skin is deeply bronzed and her black hair is in long braids, just like my doll's. She could be my friend in Havana, I think dreamily. But a moment later, her boat moves on, and I am left again to wonder when we will ever step onto dry land.

The fishermen and their families are the first to sail out to see us. But within a couple of days, the small boats that approach the *St. Louis* also carry men and women who have come looking for friends and relatives who are on board. I can see these small vessels slowly circling round and round the ship like the colorful horses from the merry-go-round in the Englischen Garten. The people in the small boats stare up at our huge decks, searching for familiar faces. The heat of the day is interrupted by shouts of joy when fellow passengers spot someone they know in a dinghy below.

"I'm here, Klara," a woman next to me shrieks.

"Tell my brother Erich that I am well," someone else shouts.

A couple of the boats come too close to the *St. Louis,* and are shooed away by police vessels that have also come from the harbor. The small crafts move away to a respectable distance, as their passengers

Relatives of passengers came out to the ship in
small vessels, like this tugboat, to greet their friends.

continue to shout greetings to those on board the ship. In between the cries of joy at spotting a loved one, there are pleas for information about when we will get off. Over and over, the same answers float up to the decks of the *St. Louis*.

"Soon," the people in the small boats reply, shouting words of encouragement. "The authorities on shore are working to get everyone ashore. Try to be patient and all will be well."

Patient! There's that word again. And even though Mutti seems calm as these days pass, a tickle of fear has begun to creep into my mind. I can't explain why I am scared. Maybe it is just the thought of sailing away from here, and being miserably seasick again. Maybe it's because none of the crewmembers have better answers for us than the relatives who circle the ship in dinghies. Whatever it is, I can feel the uncertainty, and it is growing like an icicle in my heart.

When I ask Mutti again when we will land, she waves away my question with her hand. "Soon," she says, just like everyone else. "Don't worry so much, Lisa. We have papers that will allow us into Havana. Besides, Cuba is only a temporary stop for us. Our real documents allow us to go to America. So one way or the other, we will be able to get off soon."

And still I am not convinced.

It is four days now that we have been waiting here. And I am beginning to see that I am not the only one who is worried. No one says much. People walk around the ship's decks or pause at the railing to watch the small boats that continue to circle, and continue to bring relatives out to speak to those on board. But since there is no news from the captain, the excitement has given way to doubt and now fear about what will happen to us.

Mutti and I are standing at the railing as we have been doing these past four days, saying little and watching the endless line of

Among the passengers standing at the railing of the *St. Louis* is Lisa's mother. She is at the back of the crowd, in the center, wearing dark glasses.

boats going back and forth from the shore. She is quiet, lost in some thoughts that I cannot read. And her eyes have lost the brightness that was there when she spoke of getting off the ship.

It must be over one hundred degrees here on the deck. The mid-day sun is harsh, pouring down on us with the intensity of a bonfire. I don't mind. It feels better to me than the cold and damp of Germany. Around me women try to cool themselves with makeshift fans, and men have wrapped their handkerchiefs around their necks. Many passengers look as if they are wilting, like pots of flowers left too long in the sun.

Suddenly, I feel Mutti stiffen beside me, and when I turn to look at her face, I see that she is staring at the water and pointing at a small vessel that is approaching. I follow her finger. There is nothing unusual about the motorboat. It is just like the dozens of boats that have been going in circles around our ship these past four days. A man is standing at the front of this boat. He is bald and the sun glistens off his shiny brow.

"Look, look! I can't believe it. It's…it's your Uncle Werner!" At first, Mutti is almost speechless; she is so amazed by the sight of her twin sister's husband. But almost immediately she finds her voice, and begins shouting and waving to the man on the boat. Within seconds he begins to wave back.

"Werner, Werner, we're here!" Mutti screams. She is practically jumping up and down, gesturing wildly. "He must have flown down to Havana," she says to me, still waving and dancing with joy. My Uncle Werner lives in America, in that city called Hackensack. I am so shocked to see him here, too. I watch his vessel approach as close as it can before the police boats will stop it. I am suddenly joyful, thinking that finally we will be saved.

Uncle Werner is yelling something to Mutti, and I struggle to hear him across the great divide between his boat and the two of us, so high above him on the top deck. It is several minutes before I can make out what he is saying, and his words, when they finally reach me, are not exactly what I had wanted to hear.

"I'm trying to get you off the ship," he shouts. "But it will take more time – a few more days at the most. Be patient."

I am done with patience. I've had my fill of waiting. I jump up to lean over the railing. "Take me out of here, now!" I scream. My arms reach out, imploring Uncle Werner to scale the side of the ship and pluck me off the deck.

Uncle Werner is so close. Here is the safety of our family in America. And yet, all of it seems so far away. We have crossed an ocean to get here, and these last few yards are the longest and most difficult to get past. I am so scared that we will not be able to get off. I am also terrified that the ship will leave and I will be seasick again, so nauseous I will feel like dying. Either way, I need my uncle to rescue me – now!

Mutti is pulling me away from the railing. "Lisa," she says, holding me tightly while I keep on crying for my uncle to get me off the ship. "Calm down. You heard your Uncle Werner. It will just take a few more days, that's all. We've come this far. We can wait a few more days, can't we?"

I am crying too hard to understand much of what Mutti is saying. I don't want to wait another second, let alone another day. But there is nothing I can do. As I stand weeping in Mutti's arms, Uncle Werner waves a final good-bye and the boat driver turns his small craft around to head for shore. Soon, he joins the line of little boats sailing back to the pier, and then he disappears from sight.

SOL

SOMETHING IS going on, and I have a bad feeling about it. In the days since we have been sitting out here, the mood on board has gone sour. The first morning, everyone was overjoyed to finally be here. Men and women cried and hugged each other, pointing toward shore as if it were the finish line of a great race. "We're free," they shouted. But Papa says the long, hot days and longer nights have taken their toll on all the passengers. Now, the men and women stand quietly at the railings, and stare with empty eyes at a shore that feels farther away as time goes by.

Even Mutti and Papa have joined those who stand all day and watch. My parents seem lost in their thoughts for hours on end. When I ask them what is happening, they brush my questions away, saying we will get off soon enough. But I know they are worried – the excitement of the day Papa showed us our landing documents is gone. And rumors that one of the passengers has jumped from the ship, trying to take his life, made my Mutti cry.

When it happened, we were in the dining room having lunch. Even the meals are different now. Though there still is lots of food compared with what Mutti and I had after Papa was taken away from us in Germany, there is far less than before. Platters are only half full. Jugs of milk have been replaced with single glasses. There is not even very much fresh water.

As we sat having a meal of small sandwiches, we could hear a commotion on the deck outside the dining room. At first, I thought it was the signal that we were finally going to land, and I jumped out of my chair, ready to run out the door to the gangplank. Papa stopped me. "We will be told when it's time to get off, Salo. Sit and finish eating."

I sank back into my chair, though I was itching to get outside and see what was happening. And then I waited for a loudspeaker announcement that we were finally going ashore. It never came, and soon the noise outside the dining room door faded away. We finished our meal in similar silence.

It was only that evening that Papa and Mutti explained to me that there was a disturbance on board because a passenger had jumped off the ship. "Poor man," Mutti said shaking her head. "He could have killed himself jumping from the top deck. Perhaps that's what he had in mind."

"But why would he try to hurt himself?" I asked. We were all eager to get off, but being so desperate made no sense to me.

Papa shrugged his shoulders. "He must be sick – maybe crazy – to think that jumping is a solution."

"Is he alright?"

"I think he's been taken to a hospital in Havana," Papa replied.

"His family is still on the ship," added Mutti. "His poor wife. I can barely look at her; she seems so lost without her husband."

That was all my parents said, and then they turned away, refusing to speak any more about it. I couldn't understand why that man had jumped. Even when things had been the worst for my family, we still always wanted to live. How had this man become so hopeless that the only way out was trying suicide? I could see that this had affected my parents more than they were willing to say. That old familiar look of fear had crept back into Mutti's eyes, making me wonder and worry.

That was a couple of days ago, I think. I've lost count of the days since we arrived here. Three? Four? They blend into one big blur as we continue to stand at the railing and stare at the shoreline. Small boats from the pier are sailing in circles around the ship. They carry local fishermen who have come out to stare at us as if we are animals in a zoo. There are even photographers and cameramen on these small boats, recording pictures and newsreels of our ship and us. I heard one passenger tell another that these pictures and newsreels are being shown in countries around the world. "We're famous," he said with a bitter laugh.

On the first day, the small boats came loaded with fruit, and were allowed to come alongside the ship. Several large pineapples were brought on board, and the crewmembers wasted no time having them peeled, sliced, and passed around to passengers. I ate pineapple for the first time in my life, and the memory of that sweet, juicy taste has stayed with me, one of the nice moments of these past days.

At night, the fishing boats are replaced by patrolling police cruisers. Their searchlights sweep the length of the *St. Louis* and probe the ocean, looking for any other passengers who might have thought they could also leap – either to their death, or perhaps to freedom. After the incident with the man who jumped, the police are taking no chances. There are even some crewmembers on board the ship who have started to patrol the decks at night, knocking on cabin doors to ask if everything is all right. It's as if they are also worried that someone else might try to jump.

Today, there are young Cuban boys about my age on some of the small vessels. A man standing beside me seems to know what they want, and has thrown a few coins into the water. A young boy on one of the dinghies dives overboard to retrieve the money. A minute goes by and then he bursts up from the sea, holding a coin triumphantly in his outstretched hand. Several men applaud, and then a shower of coins flies from the deck, and a half a dozen young boys dive into the water to recover the treasure. For the next few minutes, this game continues. Passengers throw coins and the Cuban boys dive into the water to search for them. We all laugh and cheer when the swimmers come up from the deep with the money clutched in their hands. But this moment passes when the police boats approach, and command the small boats to move away. The entertainment is over, and we go back to watching and waiting.

Sometimes the passengers from the ship shout questions to the Cuban fishermen who circle the ship. "When are we going to be able to come ashore?" they ask. "Do you know when we can get off this boat?"

It is hard to hear their responses. Their voices are lost in the wind and distance between the ship and their boats. But one word floats up. It is repeated over and over and it is the first Spanish word that I have ever heard. "*Mañana*," the Cuban fishermen shout, along with their children. "Tomorrow."

"Mañana!" I roll this word over in my mouth, wishing and praying that tomorrow will come now, and we will be able to land.

Along with the Cuban fishermen, there are others, relatives of passengers, who come to look at us on the ship. Then the silence is interrupted as a passenger spots a loved one below and there are shouts of recognition and quick broken conversations. The faces of those passengers light up with joy. They now have hope that they will soon be ashore with their friends and relatives. *When will we see*

The *St. Louis* passengers tried to communicate with friends
and relatives who came out in small boats to see them,
hoping there might be news about when they could land.
Sol talked to Edith through the porthole.

someone we know, I wonder each day. *When will our relatives come out to search for us?*

A small motorboat is moving swiftly past the other tiny vessels. It catches my eye. I can hardly believe it, but it has happened. There they are, I'm sure of it. I can see a familiar-looking man, woman, and young girl on board, standing in the front of the boat. The man shields his eyes from the sun, while the woman points in our direction. But it is the young girl who makes me lean way out over the rail. She is wearing a big, white bow in her hair that bounces up and down with the waves. I know that bow. Edith! My cousin and her parents are here!

"Edith!" I scream her name over and over, wildly waving my arm over my head as if it is a flag. "Up here. Edith. We are up here!" Mutti and Papa are waving and shouting also.

"Be quiet," orders an older woman next to me. "I've got my own relatives down there. And I've got important things to tell them."

She looms over me and wags her finger in my face. But I don't care what she says or how bossy she might be. I continue to shout and wave, terrified that my cousin might not see me. And finally, Edith does spot me, and she waves back and grabs her parents to also look in our direction. She is shouting something, and so are my Uncle Adolf and Aunt Frieda. But the woman next to me is right. It is almost impossible to hear anything at this distance and in the uproar of others who are also yelling to their relatives. And then, a solution comes to me.

"Look, Mutti." I point to my cousin's motorboat. "Our porthole is right there, just where their boat is floating. If we go down to our cabin and open the window, we will be next to Edith and her parents."

Mutti stares at me, astonished. "Shloimele," she finally says. "You are a genius!"

"Our hero of the day," Papa adds.

With shouts and gestures, we let our relatives know that we will meet them at the porthole, and then we fly down the stairs, six levels, until, breathless, we enter our cabin and throw the porthole wide open. The small motorboat that carries Edith and her parents is only feet away from us. I can almost reach out and touch it – touch my family. My aunt and uncle are crying with joy, as are my parents.

"I can't believe you're here," Mutti finally stammers.

"And you," my Aunt Frieda replies. "Everything will be okay," she adds immediately. "We're sure of it."

"There are Jewish organizations that are doing everything they can," Uncle Adolf tells us, even before we have asked the question. "Don't worry. A few more days and you will all be ashore with us."

I want to believe what my uncle is saying. He sounds so encouraging, and it's good to know that there are Jewish groups that are working to get us off the ship. But no one answers when my father asks why there is such a long delay. My uncle just shrugs his shoulders and Aunt Frieda looks away. *Does Uncle Adolf really believe we will get off*, I wonder. I lean further out the porthole so that I can talk to

Edith. "I can't wait to be on shore with you."

My cousin nods. "Me too. I'll show you all the sights in Havana, Salo."

For a moment I'm tempted to throw myself out of the porthole and into Edith's small boat. In a second I could be there with her, and my relatives would take me to shore. But I know this is impossible. The police who circle the ship would spot me in an instant, and I might endanger my parents' safety along with my own if I tried to escape. Besides,

Sol spotted Edith's trademark white bow from the deck of the ship.

what is it that I am escaping from? I want to believe that my uncle and the others are telling the truth. If we are patient, we will soon be able to land.

"Rose sends her love," Aunt Frieda is saying.

"But where is she?" Mutti asks.

"She said it would be too hard to see you and then go away again," my aunt replies. "But she is well, and can hardly wait for you to be on shore with her."

Mutti turns from the window to rummage through her suitcase. A minute later she returns to the porthole, carrying small gifts that she tosses to our relatives in their boat. "There is candy for you, Edith, and perfume for you, Frieda, and for Rose. It's nothing really," she adds. "I'm glad I can finally give these things to you. At least these gifts will make it to shore even if we can't…" Mutti stops and glances quickly at me. She is crying again and barely able to choke out these words. Papa is reaching his arm out of the porthole window, trying to shake hands with Uncle Adolf. Aunt Frieda is about to answer when the Cuban boat driver suddenly yells something, and their boat begins to back away from the porthole. Our time is up.

"Good-bye, Edith," I shout, waving once more as my cousin moves away, growing smaller in the window.

"We'll see you again soon." It is my uncle who blurts out these last words.

Within seconds, their boat has turned and is speeding back to shore. We are left alone at the porthole, waving and crying until we can no longer see them. I can feel a chill running through me here in the blistering heat, as if a cold wind has suddenly cut through my thin shirt. We close the window, saying nothing, and climb back to the top deck, where we go back to our old spots at the railing. And we keep waiting.

WHAT THE CAPTAIN KNEW

WHEN THE *St. Louis* first arrived in Havana harbor, the captain saw how excited and relieved his passengers were and then how doubtful and worried they became as he was unable to give them any idea of when they would go ashore. One elderly man, Max Loewe, became so depressed and frightened as the ship sat in the harbor that he attempted suicide. Max had been a lawyer in Germany who had been forced to give up his practice. He managed to book passage on the *St. Louis* for himself and his family, but just weeks before they were set to leave, Max Loewe learned that his name was on a list for arrest and deportation to a concentration camp. He went into hiding from the Gestapo, and was able to get himself and his family onto the *St. Louis*. He was terrified of returning to Germany and being arrested, and the patrolling police boats around the *St. Louis* reminded him of the Gestapo. In desperation, he slit his wrists and jumped overboard.

Captain Schroeder formed this committee of passengers
who relayed messages to the rest of the Jews on board.

Max was rescued by one of the police boats and taken to a hospital in Havana. His wife and children were not allowed to get off the ship to be with him. Captain Schroeder could understand Max Loewe's panic, and was afraid that other anxious passengers might try the same thing. He ordered his crew to patrol the ship and keep careful watch.

Captain Schroeder also decided to form a committee of passengers – five men, with whom he hoped to be able to put together a plan for dealing with the rest of the passengers if the situation in Havana indeed became hopeless. After they read the cable saying that the ship would not be allowed to land at this time, the committee members asked the captain whether he planned to sail back to Germany, something they knew all their fellow travelers on board feared. Everyone knew that if the ship sailed back to Germany the lives of each of the Jewish passengers would be in jeopardy. Most would be arrested and probably sent to one of the many terrifying concentration camps that were already being established within the country to imprison Jews and other despised groups. No one knew that better than Captain Schroeder. He assured the members of his committee that he had every intention of helping those on board, and he promised that he would do everything in his power to prevent the *St. Louis* from returning to Hamburg. Besides, he assured his committee members, if all else failed and the ship did indeed have to sail away from Havana, then no doubt the United States would step in to rescue the Jewish refugees.

Some people were actually allowed to get off fairly quickly in

Havana. The six non-Jewish passengers who were on board were among the first to be transported to land. Eventually twenty-four Jewish refugees, who, it was believed, had bought their landing papers from sources other than the corrupt Manuel Benitez, were allowed to land. Their papers were the only ones honored by Cuba.

While the passengers waited by the railings day after day, there were some dealings that were taking place on shore and on the boat. Otto Schiendick, the Gestapo spy, was finally able to make contact with his Cuban connection, Robert Hoffman. Hoffman was allowed to come on board, and handed over the plans for American submarines and destroyers, completing his part in Operation Sunshine. He transported these blueprints to Shiendick on microfilm that he carried aboard inside two fountain pens, a walking stick, and some magazines. It was a simple matter to turn these things over to Shiendick in front of the Cuban police and Captain Schroeder, who never suspected that this spy scheme was taking place right under his nose.

Meanwhile, Lawrence Berenson, the lawyer from the America-based committee, was still trying to negotiate with President Bru for the release of all the Jewish passengers. But so far he wasn't having any luck. The president wanted half a million dollars (equivalent to $7.5 million in today's dollars) in order to allow the Jews off the ship. Berenson thought he would be able to discuss this fee with the president, and perhaps lower it to something more reasonable. But President Bru refused. In a strange turn of events, however, he

HAMBURG AMERIKA LINIE

==

Die Cubanische Regierung zwingt uns den Hafen zu verlassen.
Sie hat uns erlaubt, noch bis morgen bei Tage hierzubleiben und es wird
die Abfahrt hiermit auf

10 Uhr Freitag morgen

festgesetzt. Mit der Abfahrt sind die Verhandlungen keineswgs abgebrochen.
Erst der durch Abfahrt des Schiffes herbeigef hrte Zustand
ist Vorbedingung für das Eingreifen des Herrn Berenson und seiner Mit-
arbeiter.

Die Schiffsleitung bleibt in weiterer Verbindug mit
sämtlichen jüdischen Organisationen und allen anderen amtlichen Stellen
und wird mit allen Mitteln zu erreichen suchen, dass eine Landung
ausserhalb Deutschlands stattfindet und wir werden vorläufig in der Nähe
der amerikanischen Küste bleiben.

                                    gez. Schröder
                                    Kapitän.

Captain Schroeder's announcement
informed passengers of the
Cuban government's decision to
force the ship to leave Havana.

suggested that he would be willing to continue talking about the fate of the *St. Louis* passengers. His condition was that by June 2, the ship would have to sail out of Havana's port to a distance of three miles off the coast of Cuba, the limit of Cuban territorial waters. Captain Schroeder knew he had no choice but to follow the president's orders – if the ship did not leave Cuban waters it would be forced out by the Cuban navy. The captain presumed that President Bru was satisfying those who were pressuring him to get the refugees out of Cuba, while still being able to negotiate for more money. He hadn't given up hope that he would eventually be able to land his passengers in Cuba.

Captain Schroeder called together his passenger committee and urged them to write telegrams to some important Cuban officials, begging someone to step in and rescue them. The first message went to President Bru's wife and said:

> *Over 900 passengers, 400 women and children, ask you to use your influence and help us out of this terrible situation. Traditional humanitarianism of your country and your woman's feelings give us hope that you will not refuse our request.*[3]

The cable was never answered.

On Thursday, June 1, Captain Schroeder posted a notice that read:

The Cuban government has ordered us to leave the harbor. We shall depart at 10:00 a.m. Friday morning. But our departure does not mean discussions with the Cuban government are ended. Only by leaving Havana can Mr. Berenson and his colleagues continue working. The ship will continue to be in contact with all Jewish organizations and other official bodies. They will all continue to try to arrange a landing outside Germany. In the meantime the ship will remain close to the American coast.[4]

As the crew got the ship ready to leave, an official from the Jewish Relief Committee in Cuba came on board to speak to passengers who had assembled in the social hall. He told them to be strong and not to fear a return to Germany. He said there were people all over the world who were working to make sure that wouldn't happen. His parting words were as follows:

Your committee will hear from the United States and us very often, possibly every two hours. The world is watching you. You are 'one family' now.[5]

On Friday, June 2, to the anguished cries of many of its passengers, the *St. Louis* pulled anchor and eased its way out of the Havana port. Captain Schroeder was devastated that he was letting his Jewish passengers down in this way. He was not at all convinced that the discussions between Lawrence Berenson and President Bru would lead to anything fruitful. He now believed that there was only one solution ahead. If Cuba was not going to admit the Jews of the *St. Louis*, then the United States would certainly have to come to their rescue.

Lisa

THE SHIP IS leaving Havana harbor! This morning I finished breakfast quickly so that I could catch a bit of the breeze, and look out at the Cuban shore. There hasn't been much else to do since we arrived. The days are long and hot, and most of my time has been spent at the railing, along with all the other passengers. I haven't even wanted to open a book, if you can imagine! It has been so hot that I almost can't breathe. Sleeping is impossible, even with the portholes wide open. But my appetite is back, now that we've stopped in one place and the deck is still. It's good to be able to enjoy my food, even though there is less of it than there was when we were at sea. Oma says that my cheeks are getting rounder again, and I finally have some color in my face.

Today, when I came out on deck, I saw a caravan of small boats docked at the long ladder at the side of the ship. The little boats were filled with kegs of water and milk, and big loads of fruit, vegetables, eggs, and other foods. The boxes and bundles were hoisted onto the shoulders of our crewmembers, who struggled up the ladder, and then disappeared with their loads into the dining room. I knew this had to mean one of two things. Either we needed this food to go on waiting here, or else the food was needed for the ship to continue its voyage. The next thing that happened made me realize that we are about to leave. Other boats came out to the ship – the ones carrying passengers' friends and relatives, like my Uncle Werner. But this morning the relatives did not wave and yell cheerful messages to the passengers high above them on the deck. Instead, they were crying, and shouting farewells. When I heard the people below us making their good-byes, my hands gripped the rail tightly, and my knuckles turned white. For certain we were going to be sailing away.

This is scary! We are not supposed to be leaving Havana. We are supposed to be getting off in Havana. We are supposed to be finding homes here where we will live until we go to America. Instead, as if in a nightmare, the ship is beginning to pull up its anchor and the horn is blasting a series of deep farewell notes that go right through my body. Now police boats are placing themselves between our ship and the small boats, keeping them from getting too close to us, or following us out of the channel. Why these small boats would ever want to follow us is a mystery to me. I want to follow them. I want to change places with them! The children on those little boats have a place that they can call home. They can go to school and play in a park and their parents have jobs and businesses. They can set the table for dinner in their houses, safe from the Nazis. Their homes are far from danger. What do we have? We have crates and cases of belongings somewhere in the bottom of the ship – and now, nowhere to unpack them.

"You mustn't worry, Lisa." My mother is standing next to me at the railing on the top deck. Oma has also joined us and so has Phillip. In fact, I think all of the passengers of the *St. Louis* have come out of their cabins to be at the railing as the ship sails away from Cuba. We are all watching the police boats form a barrier to the smaller vessels. We are all watching the people below us wave and shout good-bye.

"The captain posted a notice about this departure," Mutti says, telling me the news that I have already guessed.

"But why are we leaving, Mutti?"

"The notice says that the Cuban government will not allow us to stay here. It says that the captain and other people will continue to try and find a place for us to land."

I nod, though I feel shaky about everything. There is a rumbling sound coming from far below – the sound of engines being fired up. They sputter and groan at first as if they are also reluctant to leave. They have become used to the silence and stillness, as we have. But then they suddenly crank and roar and come to life. And the sea at the side of the ship begins to churn as the engines drive the water behind us. My mother takes my hand as the ship slowly moves further out to sea.

I am trying not to worry. I keep repeating things silently in my head, things I must believe. The captain has promised that he is working hard so that we will be safe. And I trust the captain. Why would he let us down? He has made sure that we are treated so well here on the ship for our voyage across the ocean — except for that terrible time when the newsreel of Hitler was shown. But that must have been a mistake, and it has not happened since. Why would he let anything bad happen to us now? Besides, Mutti keeps telling me that our documents are really meant for the United States. So if we can't get off in Havana, then surely we will get off once we reach American shores. This makes me feel better. I close my eyes and block everything else out. I must believe this.

Then I hear some sounds. I open my eyes and look around. So many of the people look scared and upset. Some are crying, even screaming. There is an elderly woman next to me who has sunk down on her knees. She is holding her head in her hands and rocking back and forth as if she is in pain. Several men are trying to lift her off her knees, but she will not budge. A small boy, younger than me, is standing next to her. He is pulling on her arm, but she is ignoring even him.

Maybe these people are so upset and frightened because they are leaving all of their relatives behind in Cuba. I feel bad for these people, but once again, I am grateful that our family is in America. Uncle Werner has probably flown back to Hackensack and he will be waiting for us there, I think, along with Aunt Edith and Arthur.

But there is something that I am very scared of right now – a fear that makes my knees shake.

"Mutti?" I ask as the ship begins to slowly pick up speed. "If the ship goes back out to sea, will I be sick again?"

Mutti shakes her head sympathetically. "I suppose if that happens, then we will be sick together," she says.

That doesn't really calm me down. "How many days will it be until we reach America?" I ask.

"It is only a day to the American coastline. But I'm not sure we will go there directly," she replies, though she doesn't explain what this means. "We may be at sea for a few days – four or five at the most."

I think about this and take a deep breath. I promise myself not to let seasickness get the best of me on this part of the voyage. I can manage four days, even five. I will take lots of deep breaths, stare hard at the horizon, and try to ignore any rocking under my feet. The reward at the end of this short voyage will be the sweetest of all.

SOL

THE SHIP IS leaving Havana. I hear the gigantic anchor chain clanking as it is hoisted out of the sea. The engines, which have been silent for these past five days, are humming powerfully, and the vibration reaches me on the top deck, moving through my shoes into my feet, up my spine, and into my arms and hands. The *St. Louis* is slowly inching its way out of the harbor.

"What's happening, Papa?" We are standing at the railing as we have been since we arrived here.

"We're leaving, Salo. It can't be helped," he replies quietly.

My father says this calmly. But all around us, people are weeping and screaming. It feels like the sound of the engines has suddenly pushed a button in all the passengers, unleashing a flood of feelings that they have kept inside all week. "We can't leave," a woman sobs. "What will become of us?" Her cries are echoed by others who also stand at the railing, their arms reaching out to shore as if they are hoping someone will pick them off the boat and fly them there. Several religious-looking men are praying loudly and swaying back and forth, their eyes closed. Other passengers stand silently. Five days

Sol and his father stood on the upper deck as they left Havana behind.

have come and gone and now we are leaving. I don't understand what is happening.

"But why are we going?" I ask. "Everyone said it would only be a matter of time before we would be allowed off the ship." At this, Papa turns away. He has no answers for me. I can see that he is just as confused as I am, yet I keep pushing him for an explanation. I can't help it. "What about the people on shore who have been working to get us off? What happened to them?" He is silent and pale. I know my father has no secret information, yet I feel he should. He's my Papa...

Even the crew, usually so helpful, are not able to offer any news. Several men stop one of the stewards, block his way, and demand some information. "This is unacceptable," one of the men shouts, shaking his fist angrily in the crewmember's face. "They can't refuse us entry." Others gather around and join in the protest, until finally the steward excuses himself, mumbling that he must get to his station and do his work. All around me, passengers go back to their praying and crying again. I turn to my father.

"Papa, what about the captain?" I have never even seen Captain Schroeder. But everyone has said that he is an honest man. And more than that, they say he cares about the passengers on the ship. He is not one of those Germans who wishes us dead. He wants to help. "Why can't he do something?" I demand.

At this, Papa looks sad and beaten. "Not even Captain Schroeder has the power to get us ashore. He can only do what the Cuban government allows him to do. And it seems they have closed this door to us."

"But our papers, Papa – you showed me the landing permit, and the number to get into America." I cannot believe that the papers, the official documents, are useless.

My father has had enough of this conversation. He stops talking, his lips set in a tight, thin line. He turns back to the railing and stares out at the Havana pier, now growing smaller in the distance. It looks as if thousands of people have gathered on shore to watch us leave this morning. Some are waving and others are shouting, though we can't hear them over the growing distance. Perhaps they are wishing us well. I wonder if they are worried about what will happen to us. Or are they cheering our departure? All I know is that there will be no "mañana." Five tomorrows have come and gone.

The shoreline is still only a few hundred feet away. But what has seemed like a short hop to safety has now become an endless distance. I realize that I had my chance to get out of here when Edith and her family came out to see us several days earlier. And now, I wish I had taken that chance and leapt from the ship onto their small boat.

I wonder if Edith knows that our ship is leaving. I wonder if she is somewhere out on that pier, standing with thousands of others and watching us sail away. If she is there, then she must be worried about us – about *me*. And she must be sad to know that I will not be joining her at her school and synagogue, or in her park or playground, running freely in the hot sun. Instead, I am here on the deck of the *St. Louis*, watching the pier grow smaller, and wondering what will become of us now.

Mutti has come to join us at the railing. She is trying hard not to show me that she is upset, but I can read my mother's face in an instant. And what's more, I can read what's in her mind.

"Don't worry, Shloimele," she says.

"But *you're* worried, Mutti," I reply, defiantly. At this, she does not respond. "Where are we going to go?" I ask. This is perhaps the most important question of the moment. "Are we going back to Germany?"

"No!" Papa practically shouts this out. "There is no chance that the captain would take this ship back there. I'm certain of that."

"But where, then?" The ship is beginning to pick up speed. A breeze has begun to drift across the deck. It provides some welcome relief from the never-ending heat.

"America will have to take us," Papa replies. "I know our number hasn't come up yet," he adds, looking directly at me and at Mutti. "But President Roosevelt will not ignore a shipload of Jews. He will show compassion. I'm sure of that as well."

I try to meet Mutti's eyes, but she avoids mine. I don't know how my father can be so certain that America will accept us. We once believed that Cuba would allow us to land and those hopes have been crushed. Will America treat us any better? This is a question I dare not ask.

WHAT THE CAPTAIN KNEW

AFTER PULLING anchor, Captain Schroeder moved the *St. Louis* to the required three-mile distance from Cuba's shore, and began to sail the ship in large circles at sea. He was hoping for a message telling him to bring the passengers back to the port, but he was worried that nothing was going to happen. There was no communication from anyone, and the supplies on board the ship were getting low. Even though he had managed to have some extra provisions loaded before the ship left Havana, Captain Schroeder knew there was only enough food for about twelve days at sea. If he could not land the ship soon, he would have no choice but to sail it back to Europe. And he had promised his passengers that he would never do this.

A couple of days after leaving port, the captain finally received back-to-back cables that gave him hope that a solution for the passengers was possible. The first cable said that nearby Dominican Republic would accept the Jews. The second message said there was still hope of landing in Cuba.

Captain Schroeder was relieved and quickly assembled his passenger committee to tell them the news of these two possible outcomes. Though they were hesitant about saying anything until a firm offer was in hand, the committee members agreed to pass the information to everyone on board. In the meantime, Captain Schroeder decided to take the *St. Louis* north toward Miami, Florida. He felt the cooler weather to the north would be a welcome change for the passengers as they waited for one of these options to be confirmed.

What the captain didn't know was how Lawrence Berenson of the American Joint Distribution Committee (JDC) had arranged these two possible solutions back in Havana. When Berenson heard that the Cuban president had ordered the *St. Louis* out of Cuban territorial

Lawrence Berenson tried to negotiate for the passengers to disembark in Cuba.

waters, he was more convinced than ever that President Bru was merely trying to save face and would eventually back down and allow the passengers to return to Havana. It was simply a matter of time and money. Berenson was ready to negotiate, and believed that he could have the ship back in Cuba within forty-eight hours.

One of the suggestions that Berenson made was that President Bru allow the refugees to stay on a deserted offshore Cuban island while they sorted out their eventual destinations. *Isla de la Juventud* [6] had been used as a prison for centuries and was located about fifty miles south and west of the Cuban mainland. (In fact, years later – from 1953 to 1955 – Cuban leader, Fidel Castro, would be imprisoned there.) Berenson thought the island would make an ideal destination for the passengers of the *St. Louis* – far away from the critical eyes of Cubans who might continue to protest the arrival of the Jews in their country. He believed that Bru was seriously considering this option.

Meanwhile, other countries from around the world were also being asked to provide a home for the passengers of the *St. Louis*. The Dominican Republic came forward at this time and agreed to offer a safe haven to the Jews for a payment of a half a million dollars. This was the same amount of money that President Bru had demanded. Lawrence Berenson was overjoyed. He thought he could play the two countries (Dominican Republic and Cuba) off of one another and negotiate the "best price" for the passengers. Berenson offered the Cuban president $50,000 (or the equivalent of more than $750,000 in today's dollars), and believed that the agreement would be sealed in no time. He even went so far as to visit Isla de la Juventud to see about getting it ready for the arrival of the passengers.

Negotiations were heating up. President Bru quickly rejected Berenson's offer of $50,000 and came back with one of his own. He would agree to have the *St. Louis* passengers land on Isla de la Juventud for a fee of $150,000 (or roughly $2.4 million in today's dollars). He added that food, housing, and other needs would also have to be paid for the period of time that the passengers were living on the island. Berenson was given forty-eight hours to accept this offer, or it would be withdrawn.

Lisa

I AM seasick again. As soon as the ship moved out to sea, the waves began to pick up and the horrible rocking started. Soon, my stomach began to churn, and I have had to crawl into the dark shelter of my bunk bed. Mutti tells me that the ship is moving up the coast from Cuba toward Florida. She says that if I come up on deck, I will be able to see the shoreline of Miami again. Mutti has not become sick this time, so she sits by my bed and talks to keep me company. She is even reading some books to me with English words that I am beginning to learn. I have learned how to say *school*, and *park*, and *please,* and *thank-you.* I like the feel of these words in my mouth as I say them aloud, and I know that if I practise, soon I will be able to say them without a trace of the German accent that I still have. But even though it is fun to be able to try English words and phrases, and learning takes my mind off my seasickness, I still don't want to get up. "Tell me when we are about to land, Mutti," I say. "Then I'll get up and walk out of here!"

Yesterday everything looked as if was going to work out well for us. Mutti came to tell me that the captain had posted a notice saying we would be going back to Cuba, and that we were going to stay on an island off the coast until we went to our other ports. I got out of bed to go out onto the upper deck. There was a lot of happy hustle-bustle, and quite a few passengers were already bringing their suitcases outside.

"We'll have some breakfast, Lisa," Mutti said, pulling me toward the dining room. "I'll send a telegram to your Uncle Werner as soon as we are off the ship. He'll be so relieved to know that we're safe." Mutti was breathless. Her eyes were sparkling and she was practically dancing with joy. "And tomorrow is your brother's birthday," she added. "Another reason to celebrate."

I wanted to be excited too. I wanted to dance with Mutti and talk about the island where we would be living until we made plans with my family in America. I even wanted to have a party for Phillip's birthday. But something told me it was too early to start celebrating. I felt nervous about that, and it turns out I was right. The ship never sailed back to Cuba, though I don't really understand why. We did not send a message to Uncle Werner. No one sang "Happy Birthday" to Phillip. The suitcases disappeared from the top deck once more, and I went back to my bunk bed. I have not gotten up since then.

Now, we are not even moving very quickly, so I can't understand why I feel so sick. Mutti says that the captain is sailing slowly in big, wide circles out at sea, and that he is waiting for one of two things to happen. Either we will sail to Havana once more, and finally land, or we will arrive in Miami and get off there. Any choice is fine as far as I am concerned – as long as it happens quickly! But when I ask Mutti when we will arrive at one of those destinations, she has no answer for me.

"No one knows yet, Lisa. But I'm sure we'll be told soon." Once more, the sparkle is gone from Mutti's eyes.

"But Mutti," I beg, "Why doesn't the captain just pick a place and go there? The captain is in charge of this ship, so why can't he just take it where he wants?"

My mother shakes her head. "I wish this could be fixed that easily, my darling. But it seems as if Cuba does not want us. And perhaps even the United States is reluctant to allow the Jews on board this ship to enter. The captain can't do anything without the permission of Cuba or America. Even the organizations that are working on our behalf are having problems.... Don't worry," she adds quickly as she sees my eyes grow wide. "I'm sure that America will eventually allow us in. And if not America, then some other country. Remember, we have our papers…"

I have stopped listening to my mother – partly because my head is pounding again, my stomach is churning, and I need to close my eyes and just take deep breaths. But I am also thinking about what my mother has just said about countries not wanting to take us – not wanting Jews. This is the first time she has said something like this.

I know we are hated in Germany. Adolf Hitler has hypnotized many German people into believing that we are horrible human beings, when really he is the evil one. I also know that not every German hates Jews. My dear nanny, Paula, would never wish us any harm. But I am afraid that there are not enough Paulas in Germany. Perhaps most Germans are also afraid of what Hitler and his soldiers will do to them if they try to help us.

But what I don't understand – what makes no sense at all – is why Cuba doesn't want us, and why America seems so slow about deciding whether we will be allowed in. Does every country hate the Jews, like the Nazis do?

All this thinking is making my head hurt worse than ever. Lying here, with my eyes closed and my stomach heaving, I remember my father's voice, how he would call me his little Liselotte. I don't think about him very often. I was so young when he died, and Mutti is both mother and father to Phillip and me now. And our Oma is always there to take care of us, too. But lately I have thought more and more about my father, and what happened to him.

If he were still alive, would he have gotten us out of Germany before all of this? If the Nazis had not discovered our "nest egg," the bank accounts where Papa was hiding money for us outside of

Germany, would we be living in a safe country right now, in a big house, with a park nearby, maybe even a park with a merry-go-round? Would we have traveled with Uncle Werner and Aunt Edith and my cousin to Hackensack, and be living there?

I will never know the answers to these questions. Papa is not with us. He never will be. It is just me, Phillip, Mutti, and Oma. And here we are on a ship that is going in circles, trying to find a place for us to land. *Going in circles*, my mind echoes. We are just like the merry-go-round horses in my favorite park. This ship is traveling in never-ending circles out at sea, with no beginning and no end in sight.

SOL

NOW THAT we've sailed away from Havana, everyone is quiet, watching and waiting, just like when we were docked near the port. But then we were excited because we thought we were getting off. Now we are numb and scared about what might happen to us. Almost everyone is silent.

I'm standing at the railing with my father. It's dusk, and the horizon is lit up like a blazing fire as the sun is about to sink into the sea. The terrible heat has lifted a bit. Papa says that's because the ship is slowly sailing north, away from Cuba. It's easier to breathe now. That's the only good thing about the last couple of days.

In the distance, there are lights shining from a shoreline close to where the sky meets the ocean. Here and there, I can make out the shapes of tall buildings, and of trees that are growing next to them. "What is that, Papa?" I ask, breaking the stillness of the evening.

"Those lights are from an American city called Miami," he replies.

Miami. I roll the word around in my mouth. It's an odd name. "Is that where we're going now?"

Papa does not answer for a long time. When he does, it's as if he's choosing each word carefully. "No one is sure where we are going just yet, Salo. Perhaps Miami – if we are lucky."

He says this last part as if he isn't sure we have much luck left. I know what he's thinking. We were lucky to get out of Germany when we did. We thought we were lucky to get passage on this ship destined for freedom. We have been lucky to be together on this voyage. But Papa makes it sound as if our luck may have run out.

From listening to the hushed discussions between grown-ups, I've figured out that America may not be eager to take in a boatload of Jews. I'm so confused about this. I thought America was a country where everyone was free to come and go, and where outsiders were welcome. The United States does not have a crazy and dangerous leader like Adolf Hitler, who hates Jews so much that he wants to hurt us, put us in prisons, and even send us away. I've heard lots of people on the deck say that the American President, Franklin Delano Roosevelt, is fair and reasonable. Why would he ignore us, or turn his back on us? But it looks like he might.

"If we can't go to Miami," for the first time I say the name of the city out loud, thinking it might as well be the moon, "then where will we go?"

Papa closes his eyes, and his jaw tightens. "I don't know anymore where we will end up, Salo," he finally says. "The captain is asking passengers on the ship to write letters and telegrams to anyone we know in America who may have some influence. The more people who know about us, the more it may help our cause. Someone is even writing a letter to Mrs. Roosevelt, the president's wife. Perhaps she will convince her husband to allow us in."

I nod. Yes, I think, writing to the president's wife is a good idea. She is a mother. I don't believe that a mother would ever turn her back on children like me and the others on board the *St. Louis*.

As we stand at the railing, my father reaches over. I can feel how strong his hand is as he grasps mine and holds it tight. Suddenly, I feel like a very little boy, when Papa and I would walk to the synagogue in Berlin each Saturday morning. We walked hand in hand, just like this, talking about my school and many other things. Here in the stillness of this evening, I am remembering this special time, shared with my Papa, strolling down the tree-lined streets. I was not afraid of anything then.

The sea is quite still. Gone are the giant, crashing waves and swaying decks that marked our voyage across the ocean. I can see boats nearby. But these are not like the small dinghies that circled the ship when we were parked in the Havana harbor. These are bigger — deep-sea fishing vessels — and they cast long nets and poles out behind them, ready to catch the large fish that swim here in the deep ocean. Now another big boat has come out to join them.

"Look," Papa has let go of my hand and he is pointing at this boat that is coming closer and closer to our ship, "there's an American flag flying from the back. Can you see it, Salo? It's the U.S. coast guard."

A sailor on board the coast guard ship is waving to us, and several passengers standing next to me break into excited chatter.

"Do you think they are waving us in?" one man asks.

"They're probably here to warn us to stay away!"

"They want to make sure no one jumps overboard and swims to their precious shore."

A moment later, the coast guard vessel moves back a distance and waits there. I reach for my father's hand once again. We are all left to wonder once more where we will end up – and when.

WHAT THE CAPTAIN KNEW

ABOARD THE SS *St. Louis*, it wasn't only the passengers who were writing letters to people in the United States asking for help. Captain Schroeder himself sat down with pen and paper and composed a letter to President Roosevelt, begging him to show compassion to the passengers on his ship.

But while it was true that most Americans hated Adolf Hitler and his anti-Semitic policies, they were not ready to welcome Hitler's victims to their country. American businesses were doing poorly in the late 1930s, and millions of Americans were out of work. The citizens of the U.S. were afraid that a flood of Jewish refugees might take away the few jobs that still existed. And if the door were opened to the passengers of the *St. Louis*, hundreds more might follow, taking jobs from Americans in need. These people were insisting that President Roosevelt keep the refugees out.

Although President Roosevelt was a caring man, he was also thinking of himself. He was considering running for president again and he needed the support of voters. He didn't want to anger them by ignoring their protests about letting the Jews stay in the U.S.

There were some groups that did support the passengers of the *St. Louis* and who wrote letters on their behalf to the president. One eleven-year-old girl even sent a letter to Eleanor Roosevelt, the president's wife. She wrote:

> *Mother of our Country. I am so sad the Jewish people have to suffer so ... Please let them land in America ... It hurts me so that I would give them my little bed if it was the last thing I had ... We have three rooms we do not use. My mother would be glad to let someone have them.*[7]

Many of these letters and telegrams were never answered, including the one that Captain Schroeder had sent. In fact, although the captain did not yet know, by the time the *St. Louis* was sailing up the coast of the United States, President Roosevelt had already decided he would not take in the passengers. He decided to follow the wishes of the voters rather than do what was right.

As the *St. Louis* neared Miami, the United States Coast Guard came out in a large boat to follow it. There are some reports that the coast guard may have fired a warning shot at the ship to ensure that it kept its distance from the Florida shore. This did not actually happen. The coast guard was there just to keep track of the location of the *St. Louis* as it sailed in circles at sea. By now, the plight of the *St. Louis* was beginning to reach other countries. Newspaper reports were being published, documenting the progress of the ship in trying to find a safe home for its passengers. One article in the *New York Times* read:

> *We can only hope that some hearts will soften somewhere and some refuge be found. The cruise of the* St. Louis *cries to heaven of man's inhumanity to man.*[8]

Many countries across North and South America such as Argentina, Uruguay, Paraguay, and Panama, were expressing sympathy for the passengers of the ship, but no one was stepping forward to rescue them. Even the earlier offer from the Dominican Republic would no longer be possible since that country was now demanding too much money for the passengers to land there. In Canada, a group of college professors and Christian ministers tried to persuade Prime Minister William Lyon Mackenzie King to provide a safe haven for the ship. It would take only two days for the ship to reach Halifax, Nova Scotia, where the passengers could enter the country through Pier 21. However, the prime minister was known to admire Adolf Hitler, whom he had met in 1937. At the time he described Hitler as "one who truly loves his fellow man." Besides, King George and Queen

Elizabeth of England were visiting Canada at that time, and the prime minister was busy hosting them. He turned over responsibility for the decision in the *St. Louis* case to his Director of Immigration, Frederick Charles Blair, a man who was known to be openly anti-Semitic. Blair had a history of stopping Jews from immigrating to Canada, and he stated that the crisis was not a Canadian problem. The Jews were not wanted in Canada.

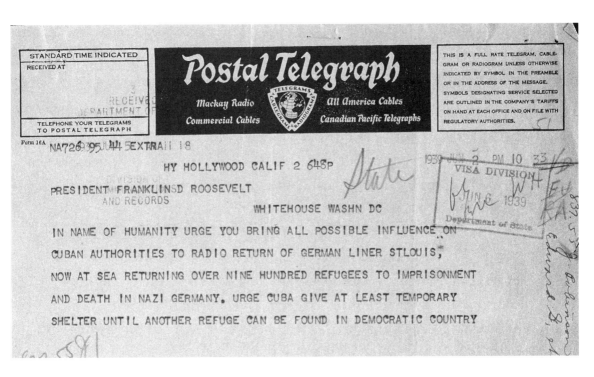

One of the many telegrams sent to President Roosevelt begging him to help the passengers. This one was sent by Hollywood movie star Edward G. Robinson.

Meanwhile, back in Cuba, Lawrence Berenson believed that he had finalized his deal with President Bru, and a message was sent to Captain Schroeder that the ship was to return to Isla de la Juventud. The captain passed this news to the jubilant passengers via his passenger committee. But their joy was short-lived. In truth, the negotiations between Bru and Berenson were going horribly wrong. Berenson had one last meeting with Bru in which the president agreed that he would accept the passengers of the *St. Louis* on the island for $150,000, but he also demanded an additional $500 per passenger in cash, an amount that would equal over a half a million dollars. Together, both of Bru's demands would total nearly $10 million in today's dollars. Berenson believed that he could still negotiate the price for the passengers down. He also claimed to have no memory of the forty-eight hour deadline that Bru had included with his offer. Once more, he seriously miscalculated the president's intentions and willingness to negotiate past a certain time.

On Tuesday, June 6, President Bru ended all discussions and refused any further meetings with Lawrence Berenson. The matter of the *St. Louis* was closed as far as Cuba was concerned, and the ship would not be permitted to return under any circumstance. On Wednesday, June 7, a shaken Captain Schroeder read this order from his head office:

Return Hamburg immediately.[9]

Lisa

WE ARE GOING back to Germany! I can hardly believe this is real. No country wants us. Cuba, America, even Canada has refused us. This time, when I ask Mutti what will happen to us, she does not even try to answer me. She just lowers her head, and I can see tears flowing down her cheeks. My mother looks as if she has given up, and I feel scared. I wish she would say something to me – say something like *America will change its mind and do the right thing*. But she says nothing.

Still, I try to understand what is happening to us. "Are we going back to our home, Mutti?" I ask her. "Are we going to live in our old apartment?"

"Who knows if our home is even there any more," Mutti finally replies. Her voice is low and as lifeless as her eyes. "It was hard for Jews before we left Germany. Who knows how much harder it will be for us when we return. More laws, more rules…"

I turn away. I don't want to hear that things have become even worse for Jewish people like us. I want to believe that we'll open the door to our flat in Munich, and Paula will be there, waiting for us. All of our belongings will go back into their old spots, just where they were before we left. And my nanny will take me to the park that I love, and Oma will play beautiful opera records for us on her gramophone. And we will go to the synagogue to pray and to listen to the cantor sing the blessings, every Saturday morning, just as we used to. Yes, maybe we'll have to sew the Stars of David back on our coats and sweaters. If that's the worst thing that happens, we can manage.

But I know very well that I am fooling myself. Mutti has said that Cuba, America, and even Canada don't want us. And I heard someone on deck laugh harshly and say to Mutti that Germany wants us far less than all those other countries combined.

"Captain Schroeder didn't even have the decency to make the announcement to us himself," Oma declared when we gathered in our cabin to talk over the news. "One of the passengers passed this awful information on. You would think the captain would make an appearance and speak to us directly." Unlike Mutti, Oma has not lost her fight. She paces around our cabin, looking as determined as ever, shaking her head and pointing her finger out in front of her the way she does when she scolds me. Oma went on to tell us how dozens of the men and women in the social hall had broken down and wept, clinging to one another, after hearing the news. "I couldn't stand to be in that room with everyone else. It was so depressing," Oma said. "I had to leave and come back to our cabin."

"I think the captain must be feeling as discouraged as the rest of us." Mutti said. "Maybe he's ashamed that he is letting us down like this."

Oma didn't respond. She just kept on pacing and shaking her finger.

When I ventured out onto the deck a bit later, I saw a group of children playing. I was too shy to join them. A wave of seasickness washed over me, so I sat down on one of the deck chairs to watch their game. There were about eight girls and boys, some younger than me and some older. Two of the older boys had taken a few of the deck chairs, overturned them, and piled them up on top of each other to create a barrier. The other children were lined up in front of the wall of chairs.

A little boy with a gray cap on his head was first in line. "Are you a Jew?" one of the big boys behind the barrier barked over the wall, like a soldier. The little boy removed his cap, nodded, and both of the big boys yelled together, "Jews are not allowed in!" The boy hung his head and walked away, while the next child in line, a blonde girl in a pink dress, moved up to the wall. The very same thing happened. The big boy who was playing guard asked if she was Jewish. When she nodded yes, he refused to let her pass.

One by one, the children in line approached the barricade of deck chairs, and one by one they were turned away. The smallest boy tried to beg his way in. He clasped his hands together and pleaded, "Oh, please, let me in. I'm just a very little Jew." But it did no good. The boys standing guard refused to let any of the children pass.

Finally, some of the children began to giggle and the girl in the pink dress ran over and shoved one of the big boys, and the game was over. They put the deck chairs back, and started to play tag, running away down the deck. I lay in the sun, breathing the cool sea air, and turned once more, to my thoughts.

No one wants us, from the oldest Jews on board to the littlest ones. We have not been allowed in anywhere. Like Oma, I wonder why the captain has kept to himself. Except for that first day when we boarded the ship in Hamburg, he has not appeared. All the grownups keep saying he must be very busy taking care of a ship this size. But like my mother, I also wonder if he feels he has let us down by not finding a safe place for us. That would be a good reason to disappear from sight.

In fact, there is hardly anyone to be seen on deck. Everyone has vanished since the announcement that we are returning to the Hamburg port. It is as if a fog has settled on the ship, a nervous, gloomy feeling, darker than the darkest storm clouds we've had at sea. The few passengers outside are walking by in small groups, silent and ghost-like. Some talk to each other in low voices, and I catch the words *Nazis* and *Germany* floating on the wind many times.

I stare out at the horizon. The sun is shining brightly on the vast ocean. There is no land to be seen in any direction. A cool breeze gusts across the deck, just enough to make me pull my sweater more tightly around me. I am shivering, but it's not because of the wind. I can't stop shaking because I am afraid. I know it won't be long before a familiar coastline will appear. Germany will loom into sight.

SOL

WE'RE GOING back to Germany. Two days ago, on June 8, a date I will always remember, Papa came into the cabin to announce the news. But I knew what he was going to say even before the words were out of his mouth. I'm not blind. I could see that the ship had turned away from land. This time we were not sailing toward Havana, or Miami, or any other port that was close by. We were sailing back to Europe. For the past two days, Papa and Mutti have stopped talking to me. Or rather, they huddle together in deep conversations, which end as soon as I come close. Well, now I know their secret. Everyone does.

"It appears that we will not have a home in Cuba after all," Papa said grimly when he entered the cabin. He paced back and forth restlessly as he spoke to Mutti and me. "I suppose that doesn't surprise me. I think I knew after the long delay that Cuba would not accept us. But I must tell you, Salo, I never imagined that America would also turn us away." My father was talking faster now, his voice rising. "I never thought President Roosevelt would be such a coward – turning his back on a shipload of innocent people!" Now Papa was practically shouting, and his cheeks were getting red. He looked at our shocked faces, took a deep breath, and exhaled slowly. "That's it then," he said more quietly. "We're going back." His eyes locked with Mutti's and a brief smile passed over his lips. "Don't worry, Pesha, Salo. We'll be fine." But his smile faded as quickly as it had appeared.

Don't worry! I have done nothing but worry since Papa told us the news and proved that my worst fears have come true. How can I help but worry? This is not what I had dreamed when we set sail for Cuba. That dream is over. And I am terrified about what might happen to us.

There is a man on the ship who has been in a prison camp. My parents whispered to me that he had been imprisoned in this terrible place, behind high, barbed wire fences, where Jewish men were taken for no reason except their religion. I don't know his name, though I have seen him walking around the decks. He has a third class cabin like ours in the bottom of the ship. He's hard to miss. At the beginning of the voyage he was so thin that his chest looked caved in. His clothes were so big on him, they were almost falling off his body. His head was shaved bald, and his skin was the color of dirty snow. No one knows why or how this man got out of that prison, and somehow managed to get passage on this ship. He began to look a bit healthier on board, gaining a little weight, growing some hair back, and he got more color in his face. But when I saw him today, he was hunched over again, dragging himself along as if he were already back in that prison camp.

"They say the Nazis are building more camps," someone told Papa grimly as we went in to dinner that night. The sky was clear, lit up by millions of stars and a thin crescent of a moon high above us. "Hitler thinks that no one really cares what happens to us. He can take us away from our homes, starve us, torture us, or even kill us. That's what will happen in those camps. No one will be safe." Mutti and Papa hurry me along, and I can see that they don't want me to hear anything else this man is saying.

As Mutti, Papa, and I sit down at our table, I ask my father, "Are we going to go to live in one of those prisons?"

"No!" My father practically shouts this, startling me.

But how does he know for sure? How can he know what will happen to us once we are back on German soil and at the mercy of the Nazis? For the first time in my life I realize that my father may not be able to protect us, and that sends a sharp shiver through me. I don't want to go to a prison camp. I don't want to be starved and tortured. I am just a young boy. It's horrible that these things can happen to grown-ups like the thin man on the ship. But how is it possible that these things can happen to children, to someone like me?

I have not spoken with Mutti about any of this. But I don't need to. The truth is, while I am close to my father, I am connected to my mother in ways I can't even explain. Maybe it's the time we spent together – just the two of us – when Papa was sent away to Poland. Perhaps it's that I am her only child, and so we have always been close. Whatever it is, I don't need to talk to my mother to know what she is feeling. Her spirits have sunk down to nothing. Her hands have begun to tremble a bit, and her eyes constantly dart back over her shoulder, as if she thinks someone is following her.

The ship has become almost silent over the last few days. The dining room that once buzzed with conversation and laughter is quiet except for muted voices and the clatter of plates and cutlery. There is less food these days at each meal, but no one cares. The movie theater is empty. Men and women sit on the deck with their heads close together, whispering. The social hall is deserted. No one dances to the music of the small orchestra that plays every night. Even the crewmembers seem different. They're as kind as they have always been, but their eyes are full of pity. They seem to know that we are headed for disaster, but they don't have any way to save us. I don't even want to play with the other kids anymore. When I catch sight of Leon, we just nod at each other and move on. The girl with the black, curly hair seems to have disappeared. It seems like a million years ago that we were jumping on deck chairs. I feel as if we are all slowly fading away, drowning.

No one really cares about what happens to us. I don't think there is a safe place for the Jews of the *St. Louis* anymore. I wish someone would take charge of this ship and save us. I wish someone would turn it around and sail it anywhere but where we are going! If I were bigger and stronger, that's what I would do. I would go to the bridge, overpower the captain, and sail this boat somewhere where we would all be safe. I would be a hero to everyone! But even as I think about this in my head, in my heart I know it is a fantasy.

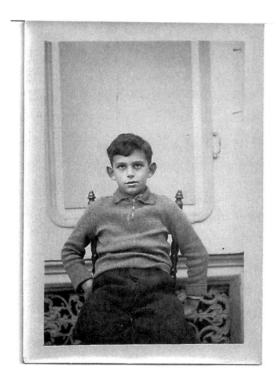

Sol as a young boy

WHAT THE CAPTAIN KNEW

CAPTAIN SCHROEDER struggled with how to tell the passengers that they were returning to Europe. In the end, he could not bear to face them directly, knowing that he had let them down in the worst possible way. He knew full well that a return to Germany likely would mean arrest and deportation to one of the concentration camps that was already in operation there. And that was enough to create a wave of panic across the ship. Both he and the passengers knew that inside these camps, Jews were being used for forced labor and were being starved, tortured, and killed. (These camps in Germany included Dachau, Sachsenhausen, Buchenwald, Mauthausen, and Flossenbürg. They were only the first in a growing number of concentration camps in Germany, Poland, and in other countries, where Jews would eventually be murdered by the millions.)

The captain met with the passenger committee members and

asked them to give the passengers the news. Following the announcement came a frenzy of desperate ideas from those on board to avoid this terrifying outcome. None of the ideas made any sense. One passenger even suggested that groups of men and women take turns jumping overboard. The captain would have to turn the ship around, he said, to try and rescue each person, thereby slowing down the return voyage and allowing more time for a solution for their situation to emerge. Of course, this idea, and all the other suggestions, was rejected. The *St. Louis* had run out of time and options. Captain Schroeder and his passengers faced the unbearable conclusion that no one wanted to save the Jewish refugees on board.

Back in Germany, the Nazis saw this as the best possible ending. Now no one in the world could criticize Hitler for his treatment of Jews when no one else wanted them either. The Nazis issued a statement saying since no one would accept "the shabby Jews," they would have to take them back and "support" them. Anyone who knew anything about the Nazis knew what that meant. The refugees would be going to the death camps.

The one person on the *St. Louis* who was overjoyed to be returning to Germany was Otto Schiendick, the Gestapo spy. He was relieved to know that he could finally deliver the plans for American submarines and destroyers into the hands of his superiors in Germany. He was already imagining how he was going to be rewarded for carrying out these undercover activities.

Meanwhile, the frantic passengers continued to send cables to important people around the world, imploring anyone they could think of to step up and help them. None of these telegrams produced any results, and once again, the refugees turned to a desperate solution. One of them, Aaron Pozner, had once been imprisoned in Dachau concentration camp where he had been beaten and starved. He witnessed public hangings of Jewish prisoners there, and saw his fellow Jews being tortured by the Nazi guards. After almost a half a year in this camp, Aaron Pozner was suddenly released, with no explanation. He was given two weeks in which to get out of Germany or be imprisoned again. With his family's help, he managed to book a third class ticket on the *St. Louis*, leaving his wife and two children behind. Aaron knew all too well what fate awaited him and his fellow passengers.

He gathered a group of men and convinced them that they could take control of the ship and sail it anywhere but back to Hamburg. On June 9th, as he stood on the bridge, Captain Schroeder was surprised to see a ragtag group of passengers, led by Pozner, approaching. They stormed in, confronted the captain, and announced to him that they were high-jacking the ship. There were a few tense moments as the captain and Aaron faced one another in this standoff. But Captain Schroeder realized that Aaron was not by nature a violent man. He was simply desperate, and willing to risk imprisonment in any country in the world for this attempted mutiny, rather than return to Nazi

POSTES, TELEGRAPHES

RÉPUBLIQUE FRANÇAISE   TÉLÉGRAMME

Indications de serv   = MORRIS C TROPER JOINTFOUND

PARIS

JOINTFUND   37

American Joint Distrib.

Committee

19 R.de Téhéran (8e)

ORIGINE   MENTIONS DE SERVICE.

N°   Timbre
date

PARIS
CENTRAL

STLOUIS NORDDEICHRADIO 784 21 16 0630

THANK YOU FOR ALL YOU HAVE DONE EXPECT TO ARRIVE

NTWERPEN SATURDAY 2 PM = CAPTAIN STLOUIS +

Germany. The captain assured the men that if they backed down, he would not report the incident. In the end, the men did back down and before they filed out of the bridge, Captain Schroeder also vowed that he would do everything in his power to land the ship in England rather than return it to Hamburg.

Left alone with his thoughts, the captain then decided that for the first time since the voyage began, he should address the ship's passengers himself, and publicly declare this promise. He gathered everyone in the social hall and pledged that no matter what, he would not return the ship to Germany. While he kept it secret at the time, the captain had devised a plan to sail the *St. Louis* close to a place called Beachy Head on the Sussex coast of England. There he would set fire to the ship and evacuate the passengers to shore. This would be his way of saving them.

Fortunately, this risky plan never had to be carried out, because a breakthrough in negotiations was about to take place.

Following Lawrence Berenson's failed efforts to find a haven for the passengers of the *St. Louis*, the person now in charge of negotiations on behalf of those on board was Morris Troper, the European Director of the American Jewish Joint Distribution Committee (JDC).

LEFT TOP: Captain Schroeder sent this telegram to Morris Troper thanking him for all he had done to save the passengers.

LEFT BOTTOM: Morris Troper and his wife

As the ship was steaming its way toward Europe, Troper stepped up the pressure on European countries and began round-the-clock discussions with those countries that had relief agencies supported by the JDC. His first contact was with King Leopold III and Prime Minister Pierlot of Belgium, who ultimately agreed to take a number of the refugees. Next, Troper contacted Queen Wilhelmina of Holland, who also agreed to accept a number of the passengers. With these two countries on his side, Troper now believed that he could put pressure on several more countries. He kept Captain Schroeder informed of his progress, but the captain shared this exciting news only with the passenger committee. The last thing he wanted to do was to raise false hope with his passengers again.

Finally, Troper was able to talk France and England into agreeing to take a number of the passengers. When he cabled Captain Schroeder with the news that all passengers would have a place to disembark the captain sank into his chair and wrote this reply:

> *The 907 passengers of* St. Louis *dangling for last thirteen days between hope and despair received today your liberating message ... Our gratitude is as immense as the ocean on which we are now floating since May 13, first full of hope for a good future and afterwards in the deepest despair. Accept ... the deepest and eternal thanks of men women and children united by the same fate on board the* St. Louis.[10]

Lisa

A MIRACLE has happened. We are not returning to Germany after all! I can hardly believe this, even as I repeat it to myself over and over. Mutti went to hear the announcement in the social hall. She raced back to the cabin to tell us all about it, and told us that it was the captain himself who had addressed the crowd. I tried to imagine what it must have been like to see the captain, in his formal black uniform with the gold braid on the shoulders, and his black captain's hat perched on his head. Few had even caught a glimpse of him for the entire time at sea. I'd wanted to go with Mutti to hear the special announcement, but no children were allowed. So I had to stay back with my grandmother and brother, waiting nervously for Mutti to return. Oma didn't help, pacing the cabin in circles.

"When the captain appeared in the social hall, everyone went silent," Mutti told us in a hushed voice, as if she was telling us a

The passengers were overjoyed to learn that they would not be returning
to Germany. Morris Troper is among them in the upper left of this photo.

mystery story. "He stood on the stage, and at first was hardly able to speak – he was so overcome with emotion."

"Then finally, he read out a telegram," Mutti continued. "It explained that everything had changed. There are four countries that have said they will take us: Holland, Belgium, England, and France. Can you imagine that? Before this, not one country was willing to offer us a safe haven. And now, four!"

Mutti's eyes were glowing brighter than I had seen in weeks, as bright as they shone when she first saw my Uncle Werner at Havana harbor. Oma laughed, with pink spots in her cheeks, hugging us all with joy. Even Phillip was grinning from ear to ear, like he'd just gotten the best present in the world.

"The ship will dock in Belgium, in the port at Antwerp," Mutti added. "From there, we will be transported to our final destinations."

"Mutti," I asked cautiously. "They won't change their minds, will they? These four countries – they won't decide to turn us away like all the others?" I didn't want to ruin the happiness that had filled our cabin, but we had been excited before and then let down.

Mutti shook her head. "No, Lisa. This time it's for real. The captain himself came to tell us!" She dragged me into the middle of the room and started dancing me around and around, until I was so dizzy I had to beg her to stop. It was then that I realized that I did not feel seasick at all. The wonderful news had chased my nausea away.

"But you haven't told us yet, Mutti," I said, nearly breathless. "Where are *we* going? Which country?"

Mutti smiled again. "England. We're going to London – and I hope, not for long," she added. "Once we are settled there, I'll contact your Uncle Werner. We'll still get to America, Lisa. I promise you."

So everything has changed again. In the days since the announcement I can see smiles once more, and children running on the decks. Everyone's talking about the news that we will be going to safe countries. I can hear the other passengers discussing their destinations.

"I would have preferred Holland," one man says. "We have relatives there. But France will be fine for now."

"We are three families here on board the ship," another woman responds. "We're just lucky that all of us are going to Belgium – to the same place."

The comments fly from one end of the ship to the other. I don't

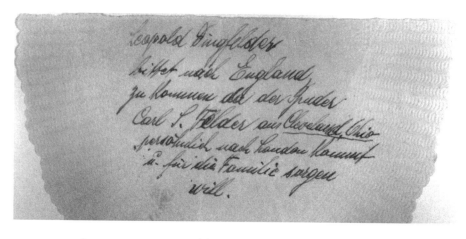

A passenger wrote this note to Morris Troper asking
that his family be allowed to disembark in England.

think it matters where we will end up – as long as we don't find ourselves back in Germany! I think England will be fine. Mutti says that Jews are not hated in England the way we were hated in my homeland. We will not have to wear Stars of David on our clothing. We will be free to walk the streets and not worry about Nazi soldiers hurting us. In England there are no laws about what Jews can or cannot do. We can do the same things as everyone else. We *are* the same as everyone else – not better and not worse.

The ship is now moving at top speed to get us to our final destination. I have my dolls with me every day now, ready to carry them with me, dressed in their finest, when it is our turn to walk off the ship. Suitcases, boxes, and crates have once more appeared on the top deck, as the first group of passengers prepares to get off in Antwerp. Oma says it will be hard to say good-bye to our shipmates. We have shared an important time in our lives, one that we will never forget. Mutti says that while we do not really know all the people with whom we've traveled these past four weeks, we are all bound together by this journey, and everything we have gone through together. And me? I feel that I have changed – it's hard to describe how. But I feel different standing on the deck, waiting for the coast of Europe to appear on the horizon. After everything I've seen on this voyage, I feel like I know some things that I never knew before, and maybe I'm a little sadder inside.

Is that what being grown up feels like?

SOL

IT'S HARD TO believe we started this journey on Saturday, May 13 – more than a month ago. Today is Saturday, June 17. I know the date, because yesterday was my birthday. But just as on Mutti's birthday, that day we arrived in Havana, there was no party, and no gifts for me. No one has had time to think about things like birthday celebrations. But that's all going to change, starting now. The *St. Louis* is steaming into port, in Antwerp, Belgium. We're so close that I can see a sign that says Pier 18. That is where we will get off the ship! Papa says this is a real miracle – there is no other word for it. Just when we thought we were lost and sailing back into the hands of the Nazis, we were thrown a lifeline. We are not going to prison camps, forced labor, starvation, torture and death. Mutti does not know how well I understand these things, but I have heard the grown-ups talking about the camps every day.

"It all happened so quickly," Papa had said, when he told Mutti and me the amazing news several days ago. But really, Papa almost didn't have to say anything. When he walked into the cabin that evening, I could see from the look on his face that things were going to be all right. Papa was smiling – almost laughing out loud with joy and relief.

"You should have heard the tumult in the social hall when the captain announced the news," he told us. "The words were barely out of his mouth when the craziness began. People started cheering and jumping up and down. Men and women cried out loud." Papa paused at this and his voice became softer. "And then, one of the passengers asked us all to quiet down," he continued. "This man walked up to where the captain was standing, and told him, on behalf of everyone on the ship, that we are eternally grateful. That we owe him our very lives. After that there really was not a dry eye in the room."

Mutti was sobbing next to me, but I knew that this time her tears were joyful ones. Her face was practically glowing. As we laughed and hugged, her happiness and Papa's calm face erased the fear from my heart. We were safe.

Now our ship is tying up at the pier in Antwerp. My family has been assigned to Belgium, so we will be among the first passengers to leave the ship. We will travel by train to Brussels, the capital city. And from there, I'm not sure what will happen to us.

"All that really matters is that we are together," Mutti reminds me.

And she is right. Papa will take care of us. He will figure out where we will live, and how.

"Besides," my father adds. "It shouldn't be long before our quota numbers are called for the United States. We'll have to sail on another ship, Salo. Are you ready to go to sea again?"

I laugh. I don't want to think about getting on another ship! Right now, I just want to watch as the long ropes are tossed to the pier, and the sailors scramble to tie up the ship. Our three cases are packed and sitting next to us. Hundreds of bags and boxes line the deck, creating an obstacle course for the crew members who are running back and forth, performing the last of their duties as the ship docks. Papa is holding my hand, just as he used to when I was little. I know this will be a day I will always remember – the day we reached safety. I don't want to ever forget even one thing about it.

"I wish you well, mein junger Herr." A steward has stopped in front of me. He reaches out his hand to shake mine. The pity that filled the eyes of most crewmembers when they believed we were going back to Germany is now gone. Today the stewards, waiters, and others who come out to see us on our way look as happy as we do.

"Danke," I reply, returning the handshake.

"Thank you from all of us," my father adds. Mutti is silent, but her eyes have once more filled with those joyful tears.

Huge crowds of people have gathered on shore to welcome us. It reminds me of the thousands who were on shore in Havana when we

Passengers on the deck of the *St. Louis* watch while the ship pulls
into the port at Antwerp, where 214 of them would leave the ship.

first arrived in the harbor. But this time we are close to the crowd. I can see the faces of the people who have gathered. I can hear the cheers go up as the gangplank is lowered into place. There are photographers here too, snapping pictures to record our landing. Was it just weeks ago that others took pictures when we sailed from Hamburg? It feels like months to me.

Believe it or not, there are familiar faces in the crowd.

"Look!" Mutti is pointing and shouting excitedly. "It's Lola and Simon. Can you see them? They are waving to us."

Lola is my Uncle Adolf's sister. It's almost unbelievable to me that there are family members here to greet us in Belgium. I raise my arm to wave to Lola and her husband, shouting until I am practically hoarse to make sure that they see and hear me. Now, I really can't wait to get off the ship, to feel solid land beneath my feet at last. I am hungry to hug my relatives. But before we are allowed to land, the officials from Belgium must board the ship and talk to the captain. I can see them walking up the gangway. They disappear into one of the staterooms, leaving us standing at the railings, yelling and shouting at the people below who continue to cheer and wave in return.

It is hours before the officials finish talking, and finally we hear an announcement over the loudspeaker. The names of the more than two hundred passengers who will be getting off the ship first are read aloud. It is not long before we hear ours. We grab our suitcases, and walk quickly toward the gangplank. Some fellow passengers look at us a little jealously, because we will be the ones getting off earliest. I can see my friend Leon ahead of us in the line, and I am happy to know that he and his family are also getting off now. Perhaps I will see him again in the days to come. I can't see the girl with the curly, black hair anywhere in the surge of people who are rushing to get off the ship. I wonder which country she will end up in.

My last thought before leaving the *St. Louis* is this. Belgium is only about 400 miles (650 km) away from Germany. But to get to Belgium we have had to travel to Cuba and back, a distance of more than 10,000 miles (16,000 km)! What a long voyage to get to a place that is so close....

I follow my mother and father off the *St. Louis* and onto dry land.

What Finally Happened

WHILE THE SHIP was heading toward Antwerp, Belgium, there was only one more decision to be made, and that was how the passengers were going to be divided up among the four countries that had agreed to accept them. Morris Troper promised to try to keep family members together if he could. Other than that, it was up to the various countries to decide which passengers they would take in. The passengers themselves had no say in this though many sent messages to Morris Troper asking to be sent to one country or another.

Not all of these negotiations went smoothly. The four countries were in fact competing for the passengers who held quota numbers for the United States, particularly those with the lowest numbers. If their stay in a host country was brief, it wouldn't be too much of a drain on that country's resources. Decisions were finally made. Belgium would take 214 of the Jewish refugees, England 288, France would take 224, and 181 would go to Holland. Those remaining in Belgium would be the first to get off in Antwerp, followed by those traveling to Holland, and finally those destined for France and England.

In 1939, as the *St. Louis* was arriving in Antwerp, no one could foresee that events in Europe were about to take such a rapid turn for the worse. World War II, which would consume the world for the next six years, was about to break out. While every passenger on board believed that their lives were being saved by the four countries willing to accept them, the truth is that their fates were determined by where they were sent. All four countries that had offered a safe haven to the Jews of the *St. Louis* eventually became involved in the war, though some were able to protect the refugees better than others.[11] All of the passengers who went to England survived the war, many eventually making their way to the United States. Many who went to France also survived, though some were interned in French concentration camps and eventually transferred to the death camps of Germany. Most of the refugees sent to Belgium and Holland perished in the death camps, after first being sent to the Westerbork transit camp. When Westerbork opened in Holland in 1939, the Jews of the *St. Louis* were among its first inmates.

In the end, estimates are that more than one third of the 907 refugees who returned to Europe perished under Adolf Hitler's campaign to rid the world of all Jews. Their deaths were completely unnecessary and could have been prevented if even one country in North or South America had stepped in to help the passengers of the *St. Louis* in the first place.

In the year 2000, a number of the *St. Louis* survivors were invited to a banquet in Ottawa held by Christian leaders who wanted to apologize for Canada's behavior toward the Jewish refugees in 1939. Among those present was a Baptist minister named Douglas Blair, the grand-nephew of Frederick Blair, the Minister of Immigration whom Prime Minister Mackenzie King had empowered to decide the fate of the *St. Louis* passengers. Douglas Blair addressed the survivors with the following words:

> *I have come to beg your forgiveness for the deep, deep wrong that was done to you. I understand very well that my name is not one dear to your heart … will you forgive me and let me call you my friends?*[12]

The surviving passengers of the *St. Louis* embraced him following his speech.

The survivors also received apologies from the American government, when on June 6, 2009, the United States Senate passed Resolution 111, recognizing the 70th anniversary of the tragic voyage of the *St. Louis*. The resolution honored the memory of all those on board, and, as they stated, recognized this anniversary as an opportunity for "public officials and educators to raise awareness about an important historical event, the lessons of which are relevant to current and future generations."[13]

Lisa
Epilogue

LISA AND her family were lucky to be sent to England, where all of those who were sent from the *St. Louis* survived the war. Getting to England, however, was a difficult journey. After leaving the ship in Antwerp, Lisa and her family boarded the *Rhakotis*, a cargo vessel that really did not have adequate accommodations for people. Lisa, along with her mother and grandmother, were given bunk beds in the hold of the freighter, while Phillip and the other male passengers had to sleep on the deck. Despite the difficult sleeping arrangements, everyone on board the boat was relieved to be there, on their way to what they hoped was a safe place.

The family remained in England for six months, first living in two rooms in London. Thick fog enveloped the city for most of that time. In fact, there were only a few days when Lisa could actually see the city! In their flat, Lisa's mother burned coal in an open fireplace for warmth and to cook. Their time in London was a far cry from the wealthy life they had once enjoyed in Germany. But the important thing was that they were safe and they were together. When the Second World War broke out in September of 1939, Lisa and her family moved to a rooming house in the Devon region, in a small town called Yelverton. It was safer to get out of London at that time than risk remaining there in the midst of the war. And while their accommodations in Yelverton were very simple, there was a massive green meadow right by the rooming house where they were staying. Horses roamed across the vast field, and Lisa enjoyed more space and freedom than she had experienced in a very long time. There the family waited until their quota numbers for the United States came up, and they were finally able to get passage to America on a ship.

That ship sailed without incident, and docked in New York harbor in early 1940. Uncle Werner was on the pier to greet Lisa, Phillip, Mutti, and Oma. From there, they went to Hackensack to join the rest of the family. Four years later, Lisa and her family moved to New York, and lived in a neighborhood called Washington Heights. Their rabbi from the Hauptsynagoge in Munich, Rabbi Baerwald, lived close by. During that time, Lisa's mother took a job in the garment industry doing sewing, often working late hours to help support her family. Oma also worked, as a cleaning lady and babysitter. Both Lisa and Phillip went to school. As a high school student, Phillip was once invited to participate in a school program that was moderated by

Eleanor Roosevelt, the wife of President Franklin D. Roosevelt. When he told her that he had been on the *St. Louis*, she responded by telling him that she was very sorry. In 1951, after Phillip graduated from high school, he joined the U.S. Army, and served on active duty for three years, and then in the reserve until his retirement in 1991, rising to the rank of colonel. Today he lives with his family in Wisconsin.

Lisa had always wanted to become an architect. But in the 1950s, women were not allowed into architectural colleges in the United States or Canada. Eventually, she was offered a scholarship to Milwaukee-Downer College, one of the first women's colleges, founded by a descendant of Harriett Beecher Stowe in the 1850s. Following this, she did graduate work at the University of Minnesota and later at Columbia University Teachers College in New York City. Lisa's journey on board the *St. Louis* affected her life in many ways, particularly in inspiring her to campaign on behalf of human rights. She moved to Canada in the 1970s, where her commitment to solving problems of particular concern to women led her to work for the Canadian Congress for Learning Opportunities for Women, and then for a program that helped those who lost their jobs when factories

LISA J. FREUND
187 Pinehurst Ave.
WA 3-8220
Yearbook Art Ed., Sen. Show, Term Council, Guidance Sq., French Club, Girls' Intramurals.

Lisa's high school
yearbook photo

they'd worked in were shut. Lisa was an active leader in Canada's National Organization of Women, and published many articles about work, women, and education.

Lisa lives in Toronto, and has two grown children and five grandchildren. She is also an accomplished weaver.

Lisa spends time at her weaving loom at home in Toronto, Ontario.

SOL
Epilogue

MOST OF THE Jewish refugees of the *St. Louis* who were assigned to stay in Belgium did not survive the war. Sol and his parents were among the lucky few who did, though their journey after arriving in Antwerp was a very difficult one. Sol and his family traveled by train to Brussels, where they lived in a one-room flat. A condition of their entry into Belgium was that the refugees were not allowed to work, and so it was difficult for the family to earn even a little money for food and essentials. On May 10, 1940, the Germans invaded Belgium and five days later they were 15 miles (24 km) outside of Brussels. Sol and his parents knew they had to leave.

They arrived in Paris in the midst of chaos. Many were trying desperately to get out, in fear that the city might be bombed by the Nazis, who were soon to be invading France. Sol and his parents fled

RIGHT: Sol holds a photo of himself as a child. He lives in Buffalo, New York.

south, almost to the Spanish border, and found refuge in the Pyrenees Mountains. They lived in a tiny village for two years, hiding from the Nazis. But in October 1940, they were arrested and taken to the Agde detention camp. Conditions there were miserable. There was little food to eat, living accommodations were crowded and filthy, and there were lice, disease, and death. Women and children were separated from the men, so Sol and his mother were in a military barracks with hundreds of others, while his father was placed in another part of the camp.

One Christmas Eve, several months after arriving in Agde, Sol and his mother managed to escape when the French soldiers guarding them became drunk, and abandoned their posts. But since Sol's father was in another section of the camp, Sol and his mother were forced to leave without him. They made their way to the small town where they had been living before their arrest. A kind and generous teacher who remembered them agreed to take them in. Several days later, Sol's father escaped and joined them. It was in this small town that Sol was reunited with Leon Silver, the boy who had befriended him on board the *St. Louis*. Leon and his parents had also escaped from Agde.

Sol's family lived in constant fear that they would be arrested again. Sol's father managed to get some work as a tailor, so they were able to buy just enough food to survive. Finally their quota number for the United States came up in the spring of 1942 and Sol's father traveled to Marseilles where he was able to pick up their visas for

America. Relatives in the U.S. sent them money for tickets on a ship called the *Serpa Pinto* leaving for New York City. This cargo ship was nothing like the luxurious *St. Louis*, and Sol was seasick from the moment the ship left until the moment it arrived in New York.

Family members were there to welcome them. Sol and his parents stayed one month in New York, and then went to Buffalo to be reunited with his Aunt Frieda, Uncle Adolf, and his cousin, Edith. They had managed to get into the United States from Cuba. Sol eventually graduated from medical school at the University of Buffalo. He served in the U.S. Army as a pathologist. He continues to live in Buffalo to this day, and is active in the community of survivors from the SS *St. Louis* who live around the world.

Some years after Sol arrived in America, he discovered the fate of his friend, Leon Silver. Leon's parents were picked up by the French police and deported to Auschwitz concentration camp. The teacher who had taken in Sol and the others after their escape from the Agde detention camp managed to hide Leon and keep him safe. But Leon missed his parents so desperately that he gave himself up to the police. He joined his parents in Auschwitz, and perished with them there.

What Happened to the Others?

Max Loewe – the man who tried to kill himself by jumping overboard while the *St. Louis* was anchored near Havana – survived. His wife and children sailed back to Europe on the *St. Louis,* and were lucky enough to be sent to England. They could not obtain any information about Max until 1940, when he was released from a Cuban hospital and managed to get to London to be reunited with his family. Max died in 1942 from a heart condition.

Aaron Pozner – the former Dachau prisoner who led the failed passenger high-jacking of the *St. Louis* – was assigned to live in Holland. He was interned in the Westerbork transit camp when war broke out. Aaron was eventually transported to the Auschwitz death camp in Germany, where he perished.

Otto Schiendick – the crewmember who was on board the *St. Louis* as a Gestapo spy – continued to work for the German secret police during the war. In 1945, when British troops occupied Hamburg, Sheiendick was there working at the Message Center for the Gestapo. In the siege that followed, he was shot trying to escape.

Morris Troper – the man who negotiated with the governments of England, Holland, Belgium, and France to take in the passengers of the *St. Louis* – continued to work for the JDC. He helped to coordinate relief efforts for Jews who were trying to escape Nazi Europe for several years of the Second World War. In 1942, when the United States entered the battle, Troper resigned from the JDC and enlisted in the U.S. Army, rising to the rank of brigadier general. He left the military in 1946 and returned to his work, helping to resettle Jews who had been displaced during the war. He retired in 1949 at the age of 57, and died in 1962.

Like the *St. Louis*, the French ship, the *Flandre*, carrying 104 passengers, and the *Orduña*, the British vessel carrying 72 passengers, were not permitted to dock in Cuba. The *Flandre* was forced to return to France where all of its passengers were interned by the French government. It is likely that many perished in the death camps during the war. The Cuban authorities allowed a number of the *Orduña* passengers who held valid landing permits, to enter Cuba. For weeks after that, the *Orduña* sailed to various South American ports, seeking a haven for its remaining passengers. The captain of the *Orduña* eventually made contact with a representative of the American Jewish Welfare Board, stationed in the Panama Canal. He managed to negotiate for the remaining *Orduña* passengers to disembark in Balboa, a town in the Canal Zone. Several of the passengers were accepted by Chile, while the rest were finally admitted to the United States.

The SS *St. Louis* – the ship that had housed the Jewish refugees for their voyage to North America and back to Europe – was badly damaged in 1944 in an attack by the British Royal Air Force. After the war ended, the ship was partially restored, and used as a floating hotel. But in 1950, it was destroyed and sold for scrap.

And what became of Captain Gustav Schroeder? Once the *St. Louis* had been emptied of its passengers in Antwerp, the captain received orders to restock the ship and steer it to New York to begin summer cruises to the Caribbean. The ship was at sea when war broke out on September 3, 1939, and Captain Schroeder did not manage to get the ship back to Hamburg until January 1940. It was the last voyage for the captain. After the war ended, Captain Schroeder tried to make a living as a writer, but he struggled financially. Many of the former passengers of the *St. Louis* sent him food and clothing to help him in his later years. Two years before his death in 1959, Gustav Schroeder was awarded a medal from the West German government for all he had done to save the lives of the passengers of the *St. Louis*. On March 11, 1993, Yad Vashem, the Holocaust memorial center in Israel, recognized Captain Schroeder as Righteous Among the Nations, its highest award for Christians who saved Jews during the Holocaust.

Wheel of Conscience, at Pier 21, Halifax, Nova Scotia,
is a memorial to the voyage of the SS *St. Louis*.

In January 2011, a memorial to the voyage of the *St. Louis* was unveiled in Halifax, Nova Scotia. The *Wheel of Conscience*, designed by architect Daniel Libeskind, is meant to raise awareness about Canada's decision to deny entry to the Jewish refugees on board. The monument is housed in Canada's Immigration Museum at Pier 21, the place where the ship would have docked if the government had allowed it to do so.

A speech about this memorial declared:

While the exhibit (will evoke) painful memories of a much less tolerant time, it is necessary to do so to ensure that a similar event never takes place again.[14]

Author's Note

Lisa and Sol were very young children when they sailed with their families on board the *St. Louis*. They both have some vivid memories of the voyage, the time spent waiting endlessly in the Havana harbor, and the anguish of the return trip to Europe. I have tried to capture those memories in this book. In addition, there were decisions and negotiations that the passengers were unaware of and that only the captain and other officials had knowledge of. I have pieced together those moments in the chapters entitled "What the Captain Knew." There are also some moments that I have added and embellished for the purpose of the narrative. While the events chronicled here actually did happen, Lisa and Sol were not necessarily present to witness all of them.

Acknowledgments

I am astounded when I come across stories from the Holocaust that are not widely known. That was my feeling as I began to research the events of the SS *St. Louis*. Its journey was one that was familiar to me from having seen the film *Voyage of the Damned* years earlier. But I was certain that it was a story that would be new to young readers. And I knew that the issue of where refugees are allowed to go to be safe from wars within their borders was one that would resonate even today. The challenge was how to bring this story to life. And then I was privileged to meet Lisa Avedon and Sol Messinger and I knew that I had found the way to chronicle this journey.

Both Lisa and Sol were gracious in opening up their homes to me and in taking me back in time to their childhood memories of growing up in Germany during the start of Hitler's reign, and their subsequent escape on board the *St. Louis*. They continue to be active in the community of people who were fortunate to survive the war after the *St. Louis*'s return to Europe, and they continue to speak widely about their experiences as children on board the ship. I am indebted to both of them, and I remain in awe of their courage, strength, and passion.

One of the things I love most about acknowledgments is having the opportunity, yet again, to publicly thank Margie Wolfe of Second Story Press for her ongoing encouragement and support of my writing. She amazes me with her knowledge, passion, and energy, and I'm grateful for her guidance and friendship. This is my eighth book with SSP and I hope there will be many more to come!

Many thanks to Sheba Meland for her meticulous and diligent editing of the manuscript. It was a pleasure to work with you. Thanks also to Carolyn Jackson for the additional edits, to Emma Rodgers for her ongoing hard work in promoting this and all of my books, to Melissa Kaita for the beautiful design, and to Phuong Truong for attending to all the business needs. I am also indebted to the Ontario Arts Council for supporting this book with a much appreciated grant.

Finally and always to my husband, Ian Epstein, and my children, Gabi and Jake Epstein, you have my ongoing love and gratitude for always cheering me on and sustaining me in so many ways.

Footnotes

[1] www.jewishvirtuallibrary.org/jsource/Holocaust/stlouis

[2] Voyage to Doom: www.paperpen.com/heritage/350/look/look2.htm

[3] Gordon Thomas and Max Morgan Witts, *Voyage of the Damned*, Stein and Day, New York, 1974, p. 176.

[4] ibid, p. 212

[5] ibid, p. 224

[6] *Isla de la Juventud* translates into Isle of Youth. It was renamed the Isle of Pines in 1978.

[7] American Jewish Historical Society website, www.ajhs.org/scholarship/chapters/chapter.cfm?documentID=303

[8] www.narrow-gate.net/jeffking/archives

[9] Gordon Thomas and Max Morgan Witts, *Voyage of the Damned*, Stein and Day, New York, 1974, p 262.

[10] www.paperpen.com/heritage/350/look/look2.htm

[11] England and France declared war on Germany in September 1939. Holland and Belgium were both attacked and conquered by Germany in May 1940.

[12] www.narrow-gate.net/jeffking/archives

[13] www.thestlouisproject.com

[14] Jon Goldberg, Executive Director, Atlantic Jewish Council Nov. 5, 2009, www.gov.ns.ca/news/details

[*] Chaim Weizmann quote on page v: Manchester Guardian, 23rd May 1936, cited A.J. Sherman, *Island Refuge, Britain and the Refugees from the Third Reich, 1933-1939*, (London, Elek Books Limited, 1973), p112.

Photo Credits

Cover photos: Sol family photos courtesy Sol Messinger, all other photos from the United States Holocaust Memorial Museum (USHMM)

page 4: USHMM, courtesy of Herbert & Vera Karliner

page 6: courtesy Lisa Avedon

page 8: USHMM, courtesy of Betty Troper Yaeger

page 9: courtesy Lisa Avedon, photo by Kathy Kacer

page 12-23: all photos courtesy Sol Messinger

page 26: courtesy Lisa Avedon

page 28: courtesy Lisa Avedon, photos by Kathy Kacer

page 30: USHMM, courtesy of Gerri Felder

page 32: courtesy Lisa Avedon

page 39: USHMM, courtesy of Herbert & Vera Karliner

page 40: USHMM, courtesy of Herbert & Vera Karliner

page 46: USHMM, courtesy of Herbert & Vera Karliner

page 47: USHMM, courtesy of Herbert & Vera Karliner

page 54: USHMM, courtesy of Fred [Fritz] Vendig

page 56: courtesy Sol Messinger

page 62: USHMM, courtesy of Fred Buff

page 70: USHMM, courtesy of Fred Buff

page 73: USHMM, courtesy of Fred Buff

page 76: courtesy Sol Messinger

page 87: USHMM, courtesy of Fred [Fritz] Vendig

page 90: USHMM, courtesy of Fred [Fritz] Vendig

page 101: USHMM, courtesy of Fred [Fritz] Vendig

page 103: courtesy Lisa Avedon

page 112: National Archives and Records Administration, College Park

page 115: courtesy Sol Messinger

page 118: USHMM, courtesy of Betty Troper Yaeger

page 121: USHMM, courtesy of Liesl Joseph Loeb

page 131: courtesy Sol Messinger

page 151: USHMM

page 162: courtesy Sol Messinger

page 166: USHMM, courtesy of Betty Troper Yaeger and USHMM, courtesy of Milton Koch

page 170: USHMM, courtesy of Dr. Liane Reif-Lehrer

page 172: USHMM, courtesy of Betty Troper Yaeger

page 177: USHMM, courtesy of Betty Troper Yaeger

page 186: courtesy Lisa Avedon

page 187: courtesy Lisa Avedon, photo by Kathy Kacer

page 189: courtesy Sol Messinger, photo by Kathy Kacer

page 195: courtesy Soheil Mosun Limited

page 205: Kathy Kacer author photo by Negin Sairafu

About the Author

KATHY KACER has written many books about the Holocaust, including six other books in the Holocaust Remembrance Series for Young Readers: *The Secret of Gabi's Dresser*, *The Night Spies*, *Clara's War*, *The Underground Reporters*, *Hiding Edith*, and *The Diary of Laura's Twin*. A former psychologist, Kathy has traveled around the world speaking to young people about the importance of remembering the Holocaust. She also addresses adults about how to teach sensitive material to young children. In 2010 she published her first book for adults: *Restitution: A family's fight for their heritage lost in the Holocaust*. Kathy lives in Toronto with her family.

Visit Kathy's website and blog at www.kathykacer.com

The Holocaust Remembrance Series for Young Readers

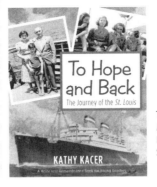

To Hope and Back
Kathy Kacer
ISBN: 978-1-897187-96-8
$14.95

Guardian Angel House
Kathy Clark
ISBN: 978-1-897187-58-6
$14.95

The Diary of Laura's Twin
Kathy Kacer
ISBN: 978-1-897187-39-5
$14.95

Hana's Suitcase
Karen Levine
ISBN: 978-1-896764-55-9
$16.95

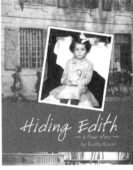

Hiding Edith - *A True Story*
Kathy Kacer
ISBN: 978-1-897187-06-7
$14.95

The Underground Reporters
A True Story
Kathy Kacer
ISBN:
978-1-896764-85-6
$15.95

The Righteous
Smuggler
Debbie Spring
ISBN:
978-1-896764-97-9
$9.95

Clara's War
Kathy Kacer
ISBN:
978-1-896764-42-9
$8.95

The Secret of Gabi's
Dresser
Kathy Kacer
ISBN:
978-1-896764-15-3
$7.95

The Night Spies
Kathy Kacer
ISBN:
978-1-896764-70-2
$8.95

www.secondstorypress.ca